THE COMPLETE GUIDE TO MULE DEER HUNTING

Tactics and Strategies for Success

SAM CURTIS

The Lyons Press
Guilford, Connecticut
An imprint of The Globe Pequot Press

The Lyons Press in an imprint of The Globe Pequot Press

Printed in the United States of America
10 9 8 7 6 5 4 3 2 1

ISBN 1-59228-204-0

Designed by Compset, Inc.

Library of Congress Cataloging-in-Publication Data is available on file.

CONTENTS

INTRODUCTION

L et me tell you about the most memorable mule deer I ever shot. I thought hunting that day was going to be about food. I'd resigned my teaching job and had plunged into full-time writing for part-time pay. So stalking down that coulee in eastern Montana with a new *Field & Stream* writer named Norm Strung was going to be a way for me to secure cheap meat to eat all winter.

Norm sent me first through the sagebrush and bull pine, hoping, no doubt, to follow behind and see that I did things right. Within twenty minutes the forkhorn was standing across the draw looking at me. I glanced at Norm. He nodded. I must have hesitated, confounded by the mule deer's continued presence in the face of my intentions. Then, Norm was at my shoulder whispering, "Aim low, just behind the front shoulder." I couldn't believe the deer was still there when the crosshairs danced onto his body. I didn't hear my shot, but the deer was suddenly dead where he had stood.

Norm patted me on the shoulder.

The skin was warm in my hand when I pulled up on the deer's stomach and pushed down with the point of my knife, as Norm instructed me to do. I followed his directions with a forced detachment from the buck that had been looking at me, focusing instead on anatomy, trying to be clinical, objective, competent. I was surprised at how quickly I had the deer field dressed and placed in the back of the truck.

And I was surprised at how quiet it was as we stood there on the plains and brushed a fly away from the buck's eye. Then Norm put his finger in the deer's blood and marked my forehead.

Deer hunting has never been easy since that day. It has never been about food alone, or antlers, or buckskin. For over thirty years now, shooting a deer has always been difficult and humbling and ceremonial. But pulling a trigger or releasing a bowstring to take an animal's life is one instant in the very complex process we call mule deer hunting. Most of that process has to do with refining hunting tactics, learning about the mule deer habitats we hunt, and discovering the habits of the mule deer living in those habitats under diverse conditions.

Our own experiences and observations in the field are invaluable foundations upon which to build our mule deer hunting know-how. But, over many years, I've learned lots of fascinating

Monster mule deer buck with doe. Getting within range of such a trophy requires stealth, skill, and a good knowledge of mule deer habits and habitat.

facts about the ways of muleys by pestering professional mule deer biologists with endless questions. So in the pages that follow you will often find references to people like Dave Pac, Ken Hamlin, and other deer researchers who have helped make me a better hunter. But, perhaps more to the point, they have given me an enduring appreciation, fascination, and respect for this wonderful creature, the mule deer.

While one of the great joys of mule deer hunting is learning about the intriguing complexities of this deer and its habitats, another dividend hunting mule deer provides is stories. And sometimes I wonder what hunters enjoy more, hunting or telling stories about hunting. So, in addition to the wealth of solid, useful, and interesting information on hunting tactics and mule deer habits and habitats that you'll find within these pages, you'll also find stories.

Assuming that some readers are whitetail hunters who may be taking up mule deer hunting for the first time, I have included sections in which whitetail habits and whitetail hunting tactics are mentioned as points of reference for understanding the differences between these two deer species and the ways we hunt them. But you'll also discover that there are times when the use of two favorite whitetail hunting tactics—stand-hunting and deer drives—are very useful for hunting mule deer.

Finally, you are going to read a great deal about north slopes, ridges, and draws, along with core and marginal habitats. If you think I'm being a bit repetitious about these things, I am. These landscape features are central to knowing how to hunt mule deer.

Sam Curtis
Bozeman, Montana

Getting to Know Mule Deer

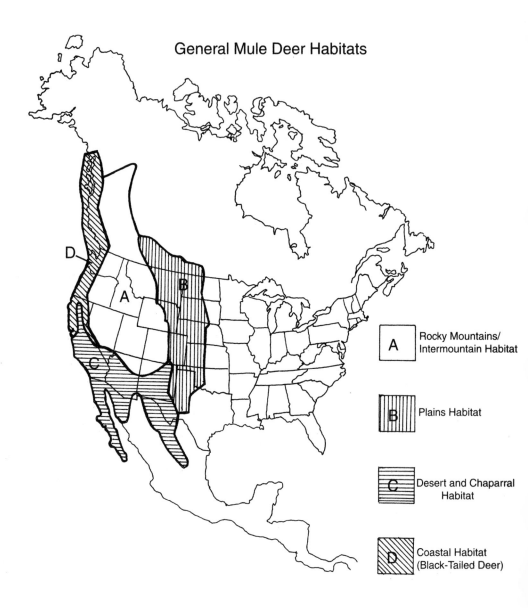

General Mule Deer Habitats

A — Rocky Mountains/
Intermountain Habitat

B — Plains Habitat

C — Desert and Chaparral
Habitat

D — Coastal Habitat
(Black-Tailed Deer)

MULE DEER EVOLUTION, DISTRIBUTION, AND HABITAT

Twenty-five million years ago a tusk brandishing, pug-nosed creature called the *Blastomeryx* became the ancestral root of what is now the deer family, including *Odocoileus hemionus*, the mule deer.

Named for their huge mule-like ears (*hemionus* means "half mule") that twitch independently, like early-warning systems, mule deer are also called "jumping deer" for their stiff-legged "stott," which catapults them into the air on all four legs simultaneously. This explosive gait, designed for the rugged terrain of the West, affords them quick uphill escapes that can leave predators panting with twelve times the exertion of a chase on level ground.

Adapting to changing niches in its environment over millions of years, the muley, as it is affectionately called, has been both tenacious and vulnerable, survivor and victim. Nowhere is this dichotomy clearer than in the heart of its domain — along the Continental Divide and on the Great Plains — where mule deer originally trickled in from the California coast to pioneer forests, sageland, deserts, and badlands.

Mule deer have become the indigenous Western deer. If you cut the U.S. in half, north to south, from roughly the eastern border of North Dakota through the middle of the Texas panhandle, you have the eastern boundary of the muley's range. From there, they inhabit a dizzying array of terrains and climates west to the Pacific Ocean (where a mule deer subspecies called the black-tailed deer resides), then north to the permafrost of Canada and Alaska, and south to the deserts of Mexico.

"The multitudinous habitats of the mule deer and the black-tailed deer subspecies are so diverse as to defy generalizations," writes Olof C. Wallmo in *Mule and Black-tailed Deer of North America*. But let's give some generalizations a try anyway.

The overwhelming bulk of the mule deer population, and therefore the best mule deer hunting, is found in what are called the Rocky Mountain/Intermountain habitat and the Plains habitat, where the largest, most highly evolved subspecies of mule deer—the Rocky Mountain mule deer—lives.

From south to north, the Rocky Mountain/Intermountain habitat extends from central Arizona and New Mexico to northern Alberta and British Columbia, then east to west from the eastern slopes of the Rocky Mountains to the Sierra Nevada and Cascade ranges. Within this habitat, "summer ranges commonly consist of a diverse mixture of coniferous forest, meadows, aspen woodlands, and alpine tundra, together

Those distinctive ears give the mule deer its name. (Gary Zahm/USFWS)

providing a rich, herbaceous flora for deer forage," says Wallmo. "Montane forest serves as winter range in many areas, but juniper-piñon pygmy forest, northern desert shrub, or shrub/grass communities are more typical winter range."

The boundaries of the Plains habitat extend, south to north, from the Texas panhandle into central Alberta, Saskatchewan, and southwestern Manitoba, and west to east from the eastern slopes of the Rockies to roughly the start of the tall-grass prairies. On the plains, the Rocky Mountain mule deer avoids the extensive flat, open grassland that makes up most of the landscape, inhabiting instead the convoluted draws and coulees, floodplains and badlands that offer the greatest variety of cover and forage all year long.

A much smaller population of mule deer, representing the desert mule deer subspecies, occupies the Desert and Chaparral habitat of southern California, Arizona, New Mexico, and Texas, where they scratch out a living in moist areas at higher elevations with broken topography.

Passing on their collective knowledge of where to find the best escape cover and forage in whatever habitat they live, and handing home ranges from mother to daughter, mule deer have evolved a social system often more functional than the frontier society that hunted the deer to near extinction during the last half of the nineteenth century.

In fact, modern game management has its beginnings in the unrestrained commercial and "sport" hunting that decimated mule deer and other game in this country from about 1850 to 1900. In the aftermath of that extravagant squandering of wild game, sportsmen and conservationists were shaken to realize that wildlife, including mule deer, was not an endless resource. States and provinces began to take action by establishing game departments, setting seasons, and imposing bag limits for the protection of mule deer and other game.

But the dustbowl days in the West in the early 1900s had a devastating effect on mule deer habitat and acted as another obstacle in the road to recovery for mule deer populations. So scarce were muleys in the 1920s and '30s, for example, that only one hunting season was allowed in Montana from 1923 until 1941.

As Western landscapes and vegetation recovered from massive drought through the 1940s and '50s, however, mule deer numbers exploded, helped on by tightly restricted hunting seasons and greatly reduced deer predator populations.

By the beginning of the 1950s, instead of being concerned about the disappearance of muleys from their native haunts in the West, game managers were worried about the overabundance of mule deer. Hunting seasons were expanded, bag limits were increased, doe hunting was encouraged, and early and late seasons were instituted, especially in areas where mule deer were damaging agricultural crops and overbrowsing their habitats. In a management attempt to keep deer numbers in balance with their forage supply, hunter harvests of mule deer in the 1960s were over 100,000 annually in prime mule deer states like Montana and Utah.

By the early 1970s, however, mule deer numbers began to slip again throughout the West. And in every decade since then, in response to environmental factors that include droughts and severe winters, mule deer numbers have taken a dive, most recently from 1995 to 1997, and then climbed back out of their hole again. But never have they reached the high numbers experienced in the mid-twentieth century.

Some hunters point accusing fingers at game managers to explain these cyclical declines. But research is teaching us that mule deer populations are, and always will be, sensitive to changing environmental factors, especially weather, habitat conditions, and predation, in addition to human management actions.

ANTLERS, VOCALIZATIONS, AND BODY LANGUAGE

Hunters have a fascination with antlers. We prize them for their points, size, and conformation. We measure them to see if they'll make Boone & Crockett or Pope & Young; we hang them on our walls. Looking at an antlered muley from a distance of 150 or 200 yards, we'll often ask ourselves: Is that the deer I want to shoot today? The answer, of course, depends on your hunting goals. You may want a trophy, or you may want tender meat in the freezer.

Here are some guidelines to determine the "Wow" factor of a mule deer's headdress.

When a mature muley has his ears laid out toward the horizontal, the distance from ear tip to ear tip is about twenty-two inches. If his antlers seem to spread beyond his ears by what looks like a couple of inches on either side, his rack is getting into the "Wow" category. Anything that looks like it is four inches or more beyond the ears puts the deer in the "Double Wow" category. That would be a rack with a thirty-inch or greater spread, and you won't see too many of those, unless you're hunting in a permit-only area or on a large private ranch with high-quality habitat and a full range of buck age classes.

In a typical four-point mule deer, look for deep, symmetrical, long-tined front and rear forks. Also, look for good mass to the thickness and bulk of the antlers. (We only count the points on one side of the rack in the West, as opposed to Eastern whitetail hunters, who usually count the total number of points.)

The biggest antlers usually sprout on a buck that is five or six years old. Beyond three or four years, a buck will develop a very black forehead, a white muzzle, and a black nose. So

Bill Barcus with his Pope and Young world-record typical buck, taken in Colorado in 1979. Antlers are symbols of social rank and dominance among male deer. (Lee Kline)

viewed head-on, his head will have a striking black-white-black appearance. And he should have a "Wow" or "Double Wow" set of antlers. Of course, any kind of "Wow" is always in the eyes of the beholder.

But what purpose do these unlikely head ornaments serve for members of the deer family, the only animals that grow them? How do they grow, and why do they fall off? What accounts for their different sizes and shapes?

Antlers are more than decorations for the deer that sport them. They are visual symbols of social rank and dominance in a group of males. They are used in ritualistic sparring matches and in sometimes fatal dominance fights over females. And there is some indication that females seek the attention of the largest antlered males because their racks indicate the healthiest and most sexually competent individuals.

Antlers are bones that grow from platforms, called pedicels, located on the skull. Covered with velvet—a variation of the regular skin on the deer's head—the growing antlers have blood vessels and nerves just like other parts of the body. However, when they have finished their annual growth—which may sprout from a third to half an inch a day on some healthy mule deer—the antler bone hardens and dies, and the velvet dries out and is rubbed off in the fall.

The cyclical timing of antler growth and shedding is a response of the deer's hormonal system to changing periods of daylight. Between March and May a hormone secreted by the pituitary gland starts the growth process. But as fall begins, increasing levels of testosterone stop antler growth and cause them to harden. After the rut, testosterone levels drop, causing the bone at the base of the antler to weaken, and the antlers are shed.

Because this pattern is dependent on varying lengths of daylight, the typical starting dates of antler growth change with the latitude. In addition, the age, health, and genetic makeup of each deer influence the antler-shedding dates of individuals in the same geographical location. For example, mule deer that were monitored in one area shed antlers over a period of 114 days one year.

Although the two antler beams of an individual male often fall off within minutes or hours of one another, one beam may stay in place for several weeks after the other has come off.

The size and number of points on deer antlers are determined by diet and age, yet it is impossible to tell how old a

male is by counting the points on its rack. Deer in healthy, uncrowded habitats produce bigger antlers with more points than deer in unhealthy, crowded habitats.

Perhaps because individual survival comes before herd or species survival, nutrition goes first into body growth, and only

Like all members of the deer family, mule deer shed their antlers each year after the rut. (Rodney Schlecht)

after that requirement has been fulfilled does it contribute much to antler growth. So any deer getting a diet lacking in protein, minerals, and vitamins during periods of antler growth may end up with pretty spindly headgear.

Given a good diet and a good genetic history, however, a buck may produce a trophy rack between four-and-a-half and eight-and-a-half years of age. After a deer is past its physical prime, its antlers do not grow as large.

Typical antlers are those with symmetry between each side of the rack. Atypical antlers—racks that grow lopsided, twisted, clubbed, or webbed—are caused by a number of factors. Genetic background may produce the same strange set of antlers year after year. Problems with calcium metabolism can cause corkscrew-shaped racks, and "cactus" antlers may result from bone tumors. A deer that is accidentally castrated may retain antlers that don't lose their velvet or fall off. Injury to an antler pedicel or a growing antler can also cause bent or misshapen points.

Whether typical or atypical, however, to produce trophy or even good-sized antlers young bucks must survive until they reach their prime antler-bearing years. Only the deer can grow the antlers, and only carefully considered hunting regulations can give them time to produce big racks.

But once the racks are grown, whether big or small, mule deer use them in a ritual called horning. Horning takes place during rut, when males thrash their antlers against bushes, saplings, and small trees. It is a display of male prowess that is intended to be heard by other males in the vicinity. And when other males hear the sound of vegetation being thrashed, they often start their own horning. When you hear thrashing, you're in luck because you've got a buck nearby. The horning process also leaves visible scars on bushes and trees, which are clear indicators that at least one buck has been in the area and may return.

A buck will often snort and hiss between bouts of horning if another buck is in close proximity. And although muleys are not as vocal as whitetails, bucks often make a strange buzzing noise when they are following closely and courting does. Either a snort or a buzz should bring you to a full stop while you scan the landscape for the deer that is making the sound.

A mule deer's body language, on the other hand, can convey social etiquette, courtship, and signals of alarm and flight. Knowing how to interpret a deer's movements—the

Sign of submission.

way it holds its neck, head, and ears, its stance, and its gait—will let you know whether to shoot fast or relax and wait for a better shot.

Although both mule deer and whitetails have similar mannerisms that convey the same meaning, whitetails are more flamboyant and showy with their gestures than muleys. This is in keeping with the temperament of the two species.

When a deer is going about its daily business, several mannerisms indicate it isn't considering anything except the task at hand. It will frequently flick its tail and ears, walk slowly with evenly spaced steps, and lower and raise its head, remaining alert, yet relaxed. This deer is not about to run off.

In the company of other deer, however, you may notice gestures that look like signs of alarm but that are, in fact, expressions of social courtesy. When moving past one another, deer often lower their heads and flatten their ears. They may also crouch and curl their tails between their legs. These are signs of submission, which may even be expressed by the dominant deer in a group. It means "Hey, everything's cool" or "Let's keep the peace."

When deer become alarmed they don't slink; they jolt to attention with their head and neck erect, ears forward, and nose pointed in the direction of their concern. A mule deer often stands in this rigid position with one front leg raised, periodically stamping the foot to the ground. (Whitetails embellish this routine by explosively blowing air through their nostrils with a loud snort.) These acts usually mean that the deer senses your presence, but it isn't exactly

Looking for trouble.

The mating stance.

sure where you are. The snort and stomp are attempts to make you move so the deer can establish your location. Such behavior indicates that the animal is very alarmed and may bolt at any second.

I've been so close to mule deer before they've bolted that I could see the hair on their rump rise and their tail stick straight out behind them. These are sure signs that your game is about to go. If you remain perfectly still, though, and the wind is in your favor, a deer in this alarmed stance may suddenly wag its tail and lower its head to a normal relaxed position.

If the deer runs off, however, certain gestures can give you a clue as to how alarmed it is. While a whitetail that is alarmed usually signals his feelings with an upraised and frantically waving tail, the muley shows his concern in his gait. A mule deer that trots off is not really alarmed. It's the stott—the stiff, four-legged bounce—that indicates a scared muley. He may travel for quite some distance before settling down.

A number of gestures are used in courting routines, including shows of dominance and submission, threats and sparring matches, and fighting postures. But the most important movement is a buck's tending posture, just before he mates with a doe. Approaching or following a doe from behind, a buck will stretch out his neck, hold his head low, flick his tongue, and avoid looking at the doe directly. This fawning posture is quite unmistakable. At this point, the buck is quite preoccupied with other matters and not at all aware or concerned with your presence. That's why some of the biggest bucks are taken during the rut.

MULE DEER VERSUS WHITETAILS

I live on the meeting grounds of mule and whitetail deer. The creek bottom by my house is filled with red-bark dogwood and hawthorn and borders a number of fields of wheat and hay. The fields, in turn, are bordered by hills, draws, and ridges covered with fir and lodgepole pine and interspersed with groves of aspen.

Mule deer come to drink at the creek and browse in the brush, but the hills and ridges are their home. Whitetails enter the edges of the forest, especially around the aspen groves, yet they are more comfortable in the brushy creek bottoms.

Over the years, my observations of these two species on this common ground have given me glimpses of the deer family's odd couple, so different in temperament and in the ways they behave when confronted by intruders. Watching them, I have come to understand that it is a combination of both their personality and habitat that influences the way these two species behave when they are hunted. By learning how each is likely to act on its home ground, you can tailor your hunting tactics to fit the deer you're after. And since these really are deer with a difference, they should be hunted in different ways. Knowing these differences will make you a better mule deer hunter.

Let's start with the mule deer. Physically, he is blocky, easy-going, tolerant, and slow to panic.

The first mule deer I ever saw was far different from any whitetail I'd ever seen. It was a young buck that I spotted on an August evening that was filled with the smell of lodgepole pine. He stood in the cool shadows and watched me with a steady stare for a good ten seconds before trotting off a short distance to resume his dinner, only half hidden from my view.

Even when spooked, a mule deer will often bound away, only to stop and look back before disappearing over a ridge. Because of this trait, some people call muleys dumb, but I think they are more curious than stupid.

Because spooked mule deer often stop to look back at their pursuers, many hunters mistakenly assume they aren't very smart.

The whitetail, on the other hand, is fragile in appearance. He's a high-strung animal; nervous, shy, and easily excitable. His movements, quick and frequent, show it. He seems always on the verge of flight.

Recently, I came upon a whitetail doe near my vegetable garden. I'd stopped still as a post before she looked my way, but she knew something was wrong, First, she stamped her right front foot; then she snorted, then she did both together. Finally, unable to stand the suspense any longer, she exploded into action, wheeling away into the brush with her erect tail beating time like a frantic metronome.

Clearly, the whitetail and the mule deer are cast from different molds. But they're also products of different environments. Whether the muley is found in barren badlands, rocky canyons, rolling grasslands, forested foothills, or alpine divides, it is the rise and fall of the landscape that is common to his terrain.

For the whitetail in the woodlands of the North, the swamps of the South, the cactus and mesquite country of the Southwest, or the river bottoms of the West, vegetation is the common thread linking these otherwise diverse locations.

Given the combination of different temperaments and different terrains, each deer employs his own bag of tricks in attempting to elude danger.

In my experience, the most revealing single instance of a mule deer in action on his own turf occurred many years ago in the foothills of Montana's Bridger Mountains. I was hiking with a friend and his dog to a rocky hogback not far from my home. Climbing the side of a wide ravine, we came upon a big mule deer buck watching us from the bottom on the draw. He was alert, but he held his ground until the dog got sight of him and took chase.

In an instant, the buck uncoiled like a spring. Up the hill he bounced with all four hooves hitting and leaving the ground in unison. Downfalls, brush, and rocks posed no problems for the big deer as he sailed over them with ease.

The dog was no match for the muley. Reaching the top of the ridge, I got a good view of the dog panting up the hill, scrambling over fallen logs and detouring around rocks. A quarter of a mile beyond, on a far ridge across another ravine, the buck had slowed to a walk and occasionally stopped to peer back in the direction he had come. The dog soon gave up the chase, and the deer went back to browsing.

Mule deer are masters at using the vertical nature of their habitat as escape terrain. First, an uphill exit places immediate physical demands on a pursuer, be it man or beast. Second, the deer is much more efficient at meeting those demands than any of his predators—including hunters.

The four-legged bounce of a mule deer is not as fast as the gallop of a whitetail, but it is very well suited to going uphill and over obstacles because it gives the deer elevation. Once this typically uphill, obstacle-strewn escape route has been negotiated by a muley, he usually finds little reason to run farther. It's not really an out-of-sight, out-of-mind attitude, for the deer will remain on the lookout for danger. However, he's not

Mule deer are adept at using steep terrain to make uphill escapes at a pace that predators can't maintain. (Rodney Schlecht)

hopelessly spooked. And he has usually only gone over a ridge or into the next draw, unless the openness of the country persuades him to put a little more distance between himself and whatever is behind him.

This over-the-ridge-and-stop routine became laughably clear a few years ago when I was hunting elk. I'd already filled my deer tag, and I was concentrating on hunting some remote ridges in the high foothills south of my home. Early in the day, I jumped a four-point muley along one of the many side ridges, and the buck bounced up through the downfalls and disappeared. After working about halfway down the ridge, I cut across the draw and climbed over the next ridge. The four-point was bedded down on a little terrace across the ravine. Again, he disappeared up and over the ridge.

I wondered if I'd see him again as I continued to hunt up and down these side ridges. And I did. Not in the next draw, but in the one beyond it and a fourth time on top of the last ridge I hunted. No elk were visible that day, but that one four-point mule deer seemed to be all over the countryside.

Given this sort of behavior, still-hunting—moving slowly and smoothly through the terrain—becomes the most effective approach to taking this species. Because of his temperament, the mule deer tolerates being stalked. Often, as in the case of my ubiquitous four-point, he moves only a short distance before slowing or stopping. And when spooked, a mule deer may pause in his flight, giving you a chance at a shot.

This habit of looking back is in part due to the mule deer's curiosity, but it is also a means of reorienting himself to your position. A whitetail will do the same thing, but because he usually does it in habitat thick with vegetation, you'll rarely observe this reorienting pause.

Mule deer tend to have a larger home range and to be more dispersed on that range than whitetails. Because of this, you have to move while hunting. And the up and down topography of mule deer country, while hard on your body, actually helps you move with less chance of detection by the deer.

But still-hunting for mule deer is more than just walking slowly through good habitat. Because a muley tends to move uphill as a means of escape, you should hunt as much as pos-

While mule deer and whitetails will both feed in agricultural fields when possible, hunting season usually finds muleys in other habitat areas.

sible from just below the tops of hills and ridges. Your silhouette will be out of the skyline, and you will have the advantage of being able to spot deer below you. Your chances of moving undetected are good because the deer will be most alert to possible danger from below, since air movements tend to be up-slope during the daylight hours.

An effective way to hunt side ridges off a main divide is to work about halfway down one side of a ridge, cut over the top, and work up the other side. When you get back toward the main divide, work around the head of the draw to the next ridge and repeat the process.

Since mule deer like to use obstacles such as downfalls as escape terrain, hunting where obstacles occur often increases your chance of finding deer. It also increases your chance of finding tough and noisy walking, so where wood roads are available, use them. Fencelines, along which cattle and horses are fond of walking, also provide good pathways through otherwise tough terrain.

While I have found still-hunting the best approach for muleys, stand-hunting fits the whitetail's temperament, his terrain, and the way he behaves when disturbed. Although a whitetail is nervous and excitable, I've found that his first reaction, in the face of danger, is to hide. Then, if further pushed, he bolts and runs, and he often runs long distances. The hiding usually takes place before you are ever aware of the deer, and that's probably why most hunters think of whitetails as runners, not hiders. However, a number of times I've watched whitetail bucks hold fast.

On one such occasion, I was resting on a forested hillside above an extensive thicket of hawthorn. I was hunting grouse, not whitetail, so deer were not foremost on my mind as my eyes casually swept over a tangle of limbs and branches. But my eyes kept coming back to one spot in the brush. It was slightly different in color and texture than the rest of the thicket, and it seemed to have more mass than the general pattern of the brush. Yet it wasn't until I'd examined the spot for some time that I could actually see what I suspected—a large whitetail buck as still as a statue and almost perfectly camouflaged.

My curiosity piqued, I stood up and walked straight down the hill toward the deer. Before I had gone half a dozen steps, the buck was on the run, not a headlong bolt from the brush, but a fast, low sneak through the middle of the thicket. Farther along the base of the hill, where the hawthorn met an irrigation ditch, the buck entered the ditch and disappeared around the corner.

Whitetails, when really pressured, will move out fast and can lose even the most determined pursuer. Their main avenues of escape are well-developed trails and runways through vegetation that appears impenetrable to you and me. But what seems impassable to us is the whitetail's line of least resistance, his well developed, obstruction-free escape routes.

I have crawled into whitetail thickets on my hands and knees and found intricate networks of these tunnel-like runways. They're miserable for a man to follow, but a deer moving close to the ground can actually run through them.

The use of a water route, like an irrigation ditch, a stream, or even a lake is another favorite whitetail tactic. It's intended to cover a deer's scent, and it may entail anything from running through foot-deep water to swimming across a lake.

All of these tricks tend to work against a hunter on the move. A naturally nervous animal on a home range that may encompass only half a square mile is too jumpy and knows his territory too well to be easily fooled by a man on foot. Because of his small range, however, the likelihood of seeing him from a stationary position is good. A whitetail is also less likely to detect you if you take a stand and hold it.

Done right, stand-hunting for whitetail is the most effective hunting technique. It doesn't depend on the right kind of weather. It minimizes disruptions in an environment the whitetail knows intimately. And it works well in both heavily and lightly hunted areas.

For the stand-hunter, careful preparation is as important as taking the stand itself. First, you have to locate the deer trails that are being used. Since deer tend to shift feeding and bedding areas throughout the year, this means scouting an area just before the season opens. By checking trails and runways after rain or snow has fallen, you can discover those routes that are currently getting the most use. And fresh rubs on nearby brush are good indications that bucks are among the trail users. Finding the intersection of two well-used runways will increase your hunting odds even more.

Once you've established that an area is being used by deer, locate your stand off the trail but within easy bow or rifle range. Also, position the stand so prevailing local breezes won't carry your scent to deer using the route. It's important to

remember that thermals carry scent upward in the morning and downward in the evening.

Your stand can be anything from a soft spot of ground behind an old stump to an intricate tree house. But be sure it's comfortable.

In areas of thick brush where still-hunting is difficult, whitetail tactics like stand-hunting can be used effectively to take mule deer.

The first time I ever took a stand, I was led in the dark to the base of a huge cottonwood and told to climb it. The rickety board steps nailed into the trunk twisted and creaked under my weight. And the narrow platform, twenty feet off the ground, seemed more like a canary's perch than a seat for a grown man. I clung there by my fingers and toes for a mere fifteen minutes before noisily descending to the ground, where I waited out the remaining hours hunkered among the tree roots.

I have since gained renewed faith in treestands—both the permanent and the portable varieties—and I recommend them over ground stands. They keep you above a deer's normal line of vision and help keep your scent out of the deer's reach. They also give you a clearer view of the surrounding terrain. And any shots fired from a stand go quickly into the ground instead of carrying long distances.

This last advantage is especially important if someone is driving deer toward your stand. A single driver, walking a zigzag route toward you, will often run deer by you that might otherwise hold fast.

While hunting along the bottomlands of the Yellowstone River in eastern Montana, a friend and I once decided to use this drive/stand technique in a particularly promising patch of willows. The flip of a coin gave me the driver's job. But since I was determined to be a part of the hunting action, I decided to make the drive in the form of a still-hunt, the way I'd hunted muleys the week before.

When the hunt was over, I hadn't seen a deer. My companion, on the other hand, had seen seven does and two bucks, one of which he was dressing out when I arrived at his stand. My mule deer hunting technique had been fruitless on those Yellowstone whitetails.

It's important to keep in mind, however, that stand-hunting and deer drives can also be useful for taking trophy muleys in the right circumstances, just like still-hunting for whitetails works well in the right kind of terrain. Knowing how each species of deer reacts in specific situations—and to specific tactics—can make the difference between a successful muley hunt and going home empty-handed.

Hunting Skills for Mule Deer

SCOUTING

As my kids used to say, "Let's pretend." It's the middle of September, and you are taking a road trip around the state of North Dakota, or Wyoming, or Idaho. The weather has been beautiful, with warm, sunny days and crisp, clear nights. In the mornings before sunrise, you have noticed mule deer, lots of them, gathered in harvested alfalfa fields across the state. You have seen them again at dusk before pulling into campgrounds to make dinner by lantern light.

Planning ahead for the opening of the general hunting season, you inquire at a local café in the town of Aardvark. You get the name of a rancher who is amenable to having sportsmen hunt on his land, and you gain permission to be at his place on opening day for what you figure will be the easiest of easy pickins.

But one month later, when you arrive back on the outskirts of Aardvark, the alfalfa fields are completely picked-over, completely dried-up, completely deerless. Unknown to you, in the time from your last visit, the deer have been forced to switch to a different diet, one containing more browse. Their fat reserves have reached a peak and their coats are thick and ready for winter. Since winter has not yet arrived, however, the deer have sought the cool refuge of thick timber on the north slopes surrounding the abandoned alfalfa fields. And you are left to wander around the fields feeling dumbfounded and foolish.

This bit of make-believe helps illustrate two things. First, your observation of mule deer in the alfalfa fields is scouting in its simplest form. Second, your failure to find deer in the same fields several weeks later is the kind of frustration you'll experience if you don't understand that scouting can be misleading and can hinder your hunting as well as help it.

In its broadest sense, scouting for deer is the systematic observation of deer habits, temperament, habitats, and whereabouts. In order to serve as a useful hunting tool, it has to be practiced on a long-term, as well as short-term, basis. Certain kinds of scouting don't have to be confined to hunting season, as long as you remember that seeing deer at one time of year

Long-term scouting will help you zero in on areas that mule deer bucks use during hunting season. (Rodney Schlecht)

doesn't assure their presence in the same place at other times of year.

Long-term scouting—the information you garner from observing mule deer over the years—is ultimately more important than short-term scouting (such as the observation of a specific mule deer bedding down in a specific spot on the night before opening day). Long-term scouting gives you the basics with which to achieve successful hunting. It teaches you about deer habits and personalities, shows you the general locations of prime habitats, and gives you an intimate sense of the lay of the land.

For example, the well-worn adage that whitetails are more flighty than level-headed mule deer has some truth to it, but it has taken years of scouting both species to teach me that whitetails are also more predictable than muleys. Whitetails have a certain routine in their use of defined trail systems that connect bedding and feeding areas. They seem to have specific routes figured out for escape if they are spooked at any given location within their habitat. Mule deer, on the other hand, are much more random. There is no predicting where they will wander. You could sit on a mule deer trail for three weeks and never see one. It's as if the muley strategy against predators is the very randomness of their movements.

Understanding the different characteristics of the two species has influenced how I hunt. Scouting has given me a better appreciation of their distinct personalities.

Where I select to hunt mule deer is also a result of long-term scouting. My decisions on where to hunt are formed partially by where I have seen these deer during past hunting seasons, where they have been at certain times of day, and how they react to varying weather conditions. But other observations taken at other times of year have also gone into my decisions to hunt new territory where I have not had a chance to observe the deer themselves during an open season.

A number of signs that deer leave are distinctive to the fall and winter seasons. Pellet droppings are the most common. During the summer and early fall when deer are still feeding on green, succulent vegetation, the droppings are soft and rather formless, and they deteriorate quickly. By the time most hunting seasons open in the fall, however, the deer have been forced to switch to a drier, more woody diet, and their droppings consist of distinct, firm pellets. These droppings may not deteriorate for several years, so concentrations of them are good indicators of fall and winter ranges.

While mule deer don't leave as many obvious rut-related signs as whitetails do, the bushes and small trees they thrash with their antlers before and during the rut are often easy to spot year-round and can be a clue to areas mule deer frequent.

One other form of long-term scouting that can be done while taking a summer hike or a winter cross-country ski is getting to know the terrain. Knowing where the ridges and draws lead; knowing the nature of their vegetation, their steepness, and their aspect; and knowing where the game trails are and where the local breezes blow are all invaluable to making wise and calculated decisions when hunting season rolls around.

Paying close attention to deer sign like droppings or tracks will make you a better hunter.
(Rodney Schlecht)

Long-term scouting, in short, is an accumulative affair, the gradual gathering of bits and pieces of knowledge about deer and deer haunts that help you understand the nature of the beast. It's the accumulation of this knowledge that gives you a solid grounding in where, when, and how to hunt deer.

Short-term scouting, on the other hand, is the gathering of information that will help you hunt a specific deer or group of deer—watching through a spotting scope as a four-point muley beds down beside a creek or observing fresh mule deer tracks in new snow, for example. Short-term scouting, combined with knowledge gained from long-term scouting, helps you make decisions on hunting tactics for specific situations.

In fact, good long- and short-term scouting should make us all successful hunters. There is a hitch, however. We have not considered the primary variables—hunting pressure, weather, and sex.

Perhaps the most overlooked influence on deer behavior during the hunting season is hunters themselves. There is no doubt that mule deer are attuned to human activity. So when the forests and fields come alive with pickups and people, the deer are going to change their ways to avoid all the hubbub. They aren't going to leave their home ranges, but they are going to use them differently. As long as the weather remains moderate, the deer will not have moved away from the general location where you saw them in September, but they won't be in the same spots or performing the same rituals you saw them do earlier.

Mule deer are often displaced from their normal haunts by hunting pressure. Along the Missouri River breaks in Montana, for example, the vast majority of hunters head for the timber in search of big muleys. Ken Hamlin, a wildlife biologist who monitors mule deer whereabouts in the breaks, claims that hunters daily drive by bucks bedded less than a hundred yards from the access road that cuts across the grass and sagebrush hillsides above the heavily-hunted timbered areas.

The muleys will still be in the general areas they were before hunting season started, but they aren't where you expect to find them. If you were to hunt where preseason scouting pinpointed the deer, you'd be looking in the wrong place. Instead, you have to ask yourself: Where, within the limits of my range, would I go if I were a deer being hunted in all the places I usually hang out?

Along with hunting pressure, weather is a major variable in forcing deer to move from one location to another during the hunting season. And the weather doesn't necessarily have to change in order to move deer. Deer will stay on their summer range as long as they can, but summer-like weather that continues into the fall can dry up forage in open areas and force deer to feed in the cover of timber or topography where shade has kept vegetation green. Continued warm weather can also force winter-ready deer onto cooler areas of their range.

But major changes in weather can have major influences on deer whereabouts, especially in northern climates. For example, near my home there is a mountain range with a sizable mule deer population. One segment of this population summers on the east slopes of the range and can be found there well into the fall, as long as there is no snow. Come the first snowfall, however, these deer do not head down the east slopes. Instead, they go up and over the divide and move down the west slopes. The weather may turn nice again with weeks of Indian summer that completely erase all signs of snow, even at the highest elevations of the range. But the deer have gotten the cue that winter can't be far away, and they have made their move.

Only careful long-term scouting will pick up this kind of information. The casual scouter, after finding deer at higher elevations on the east slopes of the mountains, would probably look for them lower down on those slopes after the first snowfall. The careful observer, however, would know that the deer were congregating in a narrow band between 6,500 and 7,500 feet above their winter range on the west slopes of the mountains. It is this kind of diligent scouting that really pays off in the long run.

And finally, there is the variable of sex. Deer know when they are being shot at. In a bucks-only hunting area, does and fawns are often quite visible through the season, while bucks may be seen for the first few days and then become conspicuously absent. In either-sex hunting districts, all the deer may go into hiding after a few days of being hunted.

Even more important, however, are the inherent differences between male and female deer. Whether they are being hunted or not, mule deer bucks use their habitat differently than does. Except during rut, they hang out in different places. In mountainous terrain, for example, mule deer bucks tend to occupy high- and low-elevation niches, while the does and fawns live in the middle elevations. Casual scouting of deer in the mid-elevations might lead you to hang out there expecting to find bucks. The frustrating results would exemplify one of scouting's little deceptions.

But persistent, careful scouting would eventually lead you to discover those muley bucks down along the foothills near agricultural land and up along the divides in alpine bowls. And it's that long-term dedication to careful observations of deer habit and habitats that is at the heart of good scouting.

Now let's move on to the key elements in spotting individual deer.

HOW TO SEE DEER

"O kay, ya see that big fir in the middle of the slope, the one with the dead top? He's bedded down on the ridgeline just to the left of that treetop. Ya see him? Right where the lodgepoles begin to get thick."

Those may not have been the exact words that Bart Yaeger whispered in my ear many years ago, but I remember my exact reply. It was an embarrassed "No"—an admission that made me feel both dumb and blind despite my average intelligence and 20/20 vision.

Bart was trying to get me to see a four-point mule deer during one of my first hunts in the West. And although I was looking right at the gray-colored buck, I was seeing only the gray of the tree trunks at his back. My companion was anxious for me to bag my first deer in Montana, yet I had to let the mule deer fall to him. He saw the deer; I saw the trees. It was that simple.

As deer hunters, our senses put us at a natural disadvantage compared to the game we hunt. Mule deer can smell, hear, and see much better than we can. In fact, our noses and ears don't do much to help us hunt. We rely almost entirely on our eyes. And we have to train our eyes to see the subtleties of shape and color of the deer we hunt within the context of their habitats. Without the ability to see what we're looking for, our hunting success (or perhaps more appropriately, our hunting failure) is in the hands of blind luck. And the task of training our eyes to see deer more readily is an ongoing process, especially when hunting new territory or country we've been away from for some time.

Shape is usually the first thing to tip us off to a deer's presence. The shape of a deer standing out in the open is quite distinctive. But nine times out of ten, your view of a deer will be partially or almost totally obliterated by the habitat. You will get only a glimpse of parts of the deer. If you can't put those pieces together to make a whole animal, you'll get to know it only as a disappearing mule deer or a fleeting set of fine antlers.

Learn to look for *pieces* of a deer's anatomy. The big, cupped ears of a mule deer are probably the best clues. Few objects found in the extremely varied habits of either mule or whitetail deer have the distinctive shape of those gently rounded ears. The leaves of deciduous trees and bushes are smaller. Twigs and branches are more elongated and angular. Rocks are too low in the natural placement of things. A set of muley ears has led me to more deer than any other part of the body. And even one ear can quickly produce an entire deer.

I once guided a teacher from Wisconsin during a fall that was discouragingly free of snow. We'd been out for the better part of three days without seeing anything, and the fellow was beginning to mutter under his breath, while I was getting apologetic. Late in the afternoon of the third day, we were following the edge of a wooded terrace that looked down into a wide

Spotting antlers in heavy cover is never easy, but looking for a piece of an animal can be the key to finding the rest of it. (Rodney Schlecht)

draw. Amid the angular shapes of trees and shrubs, one small mitten-like silhouette caught my eye. I watched it for several minutes trying to detect movement, and then the slightest sideways flick convinced me that the shape belonged to a deer.

Now the trick was to get the hunter to see the deer. I gave directions, and he strained and stared for a good ten minutes as the light got dimmer and the end of hunting hours ticked closer. Finally, there seemed only one alternative. I reached down and snapped a twig, and the deer was immediately on his feet. The hunter saw the young buck and shot straight.

Of course, all the time I watched that ear the buck's antlers had been right next to it. But antlers are deceptive because they blend well with twigs and branches. There has been only one occasion when a deer's antlers were the first things to tip me off to his presence.

I was in rolling grassland where only a few clumps of high brush served as cover. From the top of one clump stuck what at first appeared to be a dead branch. It wasn't until the branch began to move in the calm air that I realized it was the antlers of a mule deer standing in the middle of the thicket feeding on leaves.

While antlers blend in well with most vegetation, legs are more distinctive. The front legs of a deer flare out at the hooves, narrow along the shanks, flare again at the knees, and then taper smoothly out and up to the shoulders. There is nothing quite like it in their habitats. And they have a symmetry of curve, flow, and proportion that few trees or branches possess.

Rear legs are also striking in their shape. They have that angular "dog-leg" or boomerang shape that is sometimes roughly duplicated in dead snags or branches, but rarely with such grace.

Like ears, legs can tip you off to a deer's presence even when the rest of his body is hidden from view. But even something as subtle as a line can be a giveaway to a deer's whereabouts. The curve of a rump, neck, chest, back, or belly has a flare of line that most rocks and trees don't have. The most important step in learning to pick out these isolated shapes and lines is to train your eye to see the various parts of a deer's anatomy within the context of its habitat. That means knowing not only the shapes and lines of a deer, but also shapes and lines that are typical of the specific habitat in which you are hunting.

For example, mature conifer forests tend to be dominated by the straight, vertical lines of standing tree trunks interspersed with occasional straight, horizontal lines of downfalls. Shapes in this kind of habitat are distinctive but lack many curves at the level where a deer would be. Thickets, on the other hand, are

Deer are masters at blending into the country they inhabit. Without the contrast of black noses and white face patches, these bucks would be very difficult to spot from a distance. (USFWS)

characterized by a busy, irregular latticework of lines, and specific shapes are absent.

In these habitats and others, density and proportion—two corollaries of shape—are especially important to seeing deer.

A sense of density is particularly important when deer are behind a screen of leaves or branches, such as a thicket, which tends to break up the telltale lines of the animal. In this circumstance, the defining outline of the deer may be camouflaged, but the general shape comes through as a more dense area within or behind the vegetation.

Getting a sense of proportion—knowing the typical size of rocks, leaves, trees, and so on—of a particular habitat can be useful too. An incident that occurred one season clearly reminded me of this fact. I was hunting in a fairly thick stand of lodgepole pine when a shape momentarily caught my eye. At first, I dismissed it as a downfall, but then I decided to look at it more carefully through binoculars. It still looked like a log in those dark shadows, but it was a *big* log, much bigger than any of the trees in the area. Finally, after taking a few slow steps backward, I saw the light rump patch of a mule deer attached to the end of what had looked very loglike until I saw it *in relation to* other trees in that habitat.

While it was a sense of proportion that kept me from passing up that mule deer, it was color that became the positive identifying feature. Although the color of deer is not as revealing as shape, it's very important when taken with shape.

Mule deer tend to blend in with the color of their habitat. Their coats appear grayish-brown during the winter and where their habitats are drabber and more open. But they are more reddish-brown and darker in the summer and in habitats that are wetter and more shaded.

Deer also seem to have a certain chameleon-like quality to their coats. One fall I watched five muleys step out of a gray hawthorn thicket from which they seemed to just materialize. One after another, they popped into existence like magical cartoon figures. Once detached from the thicket, however, their coats—which had so perfectly blended with the color of the hawthorn bark only moments earlier—suddenly seemed to take on the tawny coloration of the wheatfield they had entered.

Whitetail hunters seemingly have an advantage over mule deer hunters in identifying prey from behind due to the distinctive tails they carry, which look like white flags waving in the distance. But to a hunter it looks more like a thumbed nose than a flagged tail for all the good it does in letting him know of a deer's presence *before* the deer knows of his and takes off. But even with their tails down, both whitetails and muleys have distinctive white rump patches. The mule deer has a dark tip on a white tail, making the rump patch look like a circle of snow with just half a footprint at the bottom.

Mule deer also have white on their bellies, on the insides of their legs, on their necks and muzzles, and inside their ears. In terms of visibility for the hunter, these areas are small, but they are generally in contrast to the colors of deer habitats when there is no snow on the ground.

On one occasion, I'd been hunting some high draws that still had patches of snow from an earlier storm. I'd been so conditioned to seeing white spots among the trees that I didn't think twice about a small patch of white on a lower slope as I headed home. Then I did a quick double take. The lower slopes seemed to be completely snow-free except for that one patch—that one white rump patch of a mule deer buck.

While the gray hair of a deer's coat is difficult to see without snow on the ground, you can pick it out, even in a drab setting. It's a matter of tuning in to texture. Just as density is a corollary of shape, texture is a corollary of color. Seen from behind a curtain of gray branches, the gray color of deer is difficult to distinguish. But the grays of the bark and the grays of the hair are different in texture. And an eye trained to look for these subtle differences will see more deer in the course of a season.

I'll never forget the crisp October morning I sat at the base of a big fir and looked down into a tangle of brush while I waited for a local mule deer buck to appear. I was convinced that this thicket was his home, and I knew he'd have to make a move eventually. I hadn't been paying much attention to the brush directly below me, but as the morning wore on my eyes kept wandering back to a patch of tangled branches that seemed different from the rest. It was a difference I can only describe as one of texture. And the more I looked, the more the texture began to take shape, until the shape became a deer, holding fast right at my feet.

Of course, while stand-hunting you have a chance to look over the surrounding habitat very carefully, and this certainly is to your advantage. But when still-hunting—by this I mean hunting very slowly on foot—you have to learn to *systematically* scan the landscape for telltale glimpses of deer. (With the typical spot-and-stalk technique used by most mule deer hunters, this becomes particularly important.) Each step gives you a new perspec-

Even in fairly open terrain, mule deer have an uncanny knack for hiding themselves. (Rodney Schlecht)

tive on the terrain. And only by sweeping your eyes across your entire field of vision can you check out all the possible places a deer may be. However, a lot of head and body movement on your part will only alert deer to your presence. So let your eyes do most of the work.

Hunting in timber, you'll find the best lines of vision confined to "avenues" or "hallways" through the trees. These are often narrow, but just as often these are the places where you'll glimpse the color or shape that betrays the presence of a mule deer.

In hilly terrain, I scan from upslope down. Assuming that most spooked deer are going to head uphill, these upslope deer will be the ones I'll have in my sight for the shortest time, if they bolt.

In flat terrain, I usually start scanning in the direction the wind is blowing, under the theory that deer in this direction will be the first to catch my scent.

The important thing is to start at one extreme of your field of vision and scan through an entire uninterrupted arc to the other extreme. Once you start letting your eyes jump around, you start missing spots in the landscape that might very well hold deer.

In order to keep your eyes on the places where the deer may be, you have to keep them off the ground at your feet. This means learning to feel your way with those feet. Every few steps a quick glance at the ground should be enough to spot any major obstacles. The rest of the spotting can be done by feel. It means moving your feet very slowly and placing them down with a light pressure that can detect twigs and branches, stumps and rocks before you snap them or trip over them.

Aids to your eyesight can also improve your chances of seeing deer. Certainly, if you see better with eyeglasses, wear them. And even hunters with excellent vision will find sunglasses make a big difference in locating deer on a bright day with snow on the ground.

Rifle scopes are good once you have located a deer you want to shoot, but I wouldn't recommend them for scanning or "glassing" as it's often called. It means pointing your rifle at unidentified objects, and it means making a lot of unnecessary movement with body and rifle that deer can detect. You're better off using a pair of good binoculars—ones that offer good definition and high relative brightness. Keep the binoculars on a short strap around your neck where they're out of the way of rifle movement but where they can easily be raised to your eyes.

Speaking of unidentified objects, *never* shoot at a shape, line, color, or texture until you have positively attached it to the game you are after. Make sure that what you have an eye on is indeed a mule deer.

THE LIGHT AND DARK OF DEER HUNTING

The knoll seemed like an ideal place to sit for the last hour of mule deer hunting that day. To the left, I could look out across a clearing surrounded by thickets; to the right, an aspen draw led down to the opening from the edge of a fir forest. Deer on the move to evening feeding grounds might very well skirt or cross the clearing or come down through the wooded draw from daytime bedding grounds higher up in the hills.

But there was a glitch in my choice of a place to wait. As the sun set and the shadows lengthened, I alternated my gaze between the opening and the forested draw. While it was still relatively light out in the clearing, the draw darkened quickly once the sun went down. And I found it increasingly difficult for my eyes to transition quickly from light to dark landscape and back again. It seemed to take thirty seconds or so for my eyes to adjust to a different light intensity before I could see things clearly and well defined.

Unfortunately, it was during one of those periods of acclimation that a large mule deer walked down through the draw.

Squinting and leaning farther into my rifle scope, I could see the buck only well enough to have regrets as he disappeared over the far shoulder of the draw.

One of the details of mule deer hunting that we tend to overlook is the matter of light—and the lack of light—we hunt in. Within the hour straddling sunrise or sunset, we can be hunting in full sunlight or in almost total darkness. One minute our shadows can loom like giants across the landscape, and fifteen minutes later we can be straining to see antlers on a mule deer only fifty yards away. Fortunately, there are things you can do to see deer better when the light is low and to be seen by deer less when the light is high.

The iris of your eye serves the same function as the diaphragm in a camera: When adjusted properly, it lets in the right amount of light for a clear, detailed image of what you're looking at. But when too much or too little light is let in, the image is either washed out and blurry or dark and poorly defined.

The problem I was having on the knoll that autumn evening was caused by sudden shifts in the amount of light available to my eyes and the need for my irises to adjust to these shifts. I'm learning that the older I get, the longer this adjustment and acclimation period takes. But anyone who has stepped from a darkened matinee movie theater into the bright light of day knows that even the best and youngest eyes need some time to adjust to sudden changes in light.

For that reason, your choice of where to hunt muleys should take into consideration large differences in light inten-

This buck stands out clearly in the sunlight, but if he steps into the dark forest behind him, he'll be much tougher to see.

sity, especially for early morning and late afternoon hunting. Avoid places (like the knoll I sat on) where your vision must make constant shifts between light and dark areas of the landscape. You are much better off focusing your eyes on one area, even if that spot is darker than the surrounding landscape. The important thing is that your eyes will become acclimated to the low light, and you'll be able to distinguish forms and movements clearly.

In any low-light situation, however, you'll want to give your eyes the benefit of all the light that's available. So be sure to take off your brimmed cap.

Let me explain. Not long ago, I was hunting with a guy who wears a Chicago Cubs baseball cap as a kind of semi-permanent fixture down around his bushy eyebrows. We were sitting on the side of a hill looking down into a thicket. Shortly after the sun went down, Stan started fidgeting and mumbling about it being too dark to hunt. But a check of my watch showed that we still had a good twenty minutes of hunting time; I whispered this news to Stan as I plucked off his hat.

Well, you'd have thought he was having a religious revelation. "There's the light! I can see," he chortled at himself and his baseball cap. And we both started to laugh loud enough to ruin what hunting time we had left.

Stan still doesn't take his hat off when he eats, but he does take it off when he's hunting deer at dawn or dusk. Try it. It's amazing how much more light you'll let into your eyes and how much better you'll see in low light.

There is one low-light situation where your hat will come in handy, however. If the best mule deer hunting conditions call for looking into a bright sky above a shadowed landscape, the contrast in the light intensities will make seeing things in the shadows difficult. In this case, a brimmed cap can shade out the bright horizon and let your eyes adjust to the darker terrain.

Another handy low-light trick is to look for good muley habitat that may hold snow cover while surrounding areas remain snow-free. Shaded draws and woodlands along streams are travel corridors mule deer often use at dawn and dusk while moving from bedding to feeding sites. These are also areas that may hold snow longer than open areas. The reflected light of the snow not only lightens these areas considerably, but the snow also acts as a helpful background against which the silhouette of deer can be seen very clearly.

Then there is the matter of binoculars. The use of the right binoculars in low light can actually cast a brighter light on your subject. In binocular terminology, the amount of light the binocular transmits to your eyes is called the "exit pupil." It is expressed in millimeters by dividing the power of the binoculars into the objective lens diameter. So a 7 × 50 binocular has an exit pupil of 7.1 (50 divided by 7). This is considered a good exit pupil rating for low-light viewing. It has 43 percent more light-gathering power than a standard 7 × 35 binocular, and it will let you see muleys much more clearly before sunrise and after sunset.

So much for the "dark" of mule deer hunting. There's also the "light" to consider. And it's the bright, low light of the sun just coming over a hill or just about to set behind it that alerts a deer to a hunter's presence faster than just about anything else.

I will always remember the frosty morning I caught a glimpse of a big buck as he ambled to the top of a nearby ridge and then was gone. It was clear that the deer was not spooked; he was in no hurry. So I hotfooted it up the hill and peered over the other side. The buck was feeding with his back to me, but he was partially obscured by some bushes. If I could move just ten yards down the hill, I knew I would get a clear shot at him. The wind was in my favor, the buck was preoccupied, and when he did look up from his feeding, his gaze was not in my direction.

I inched down the hill, watching where I put each step and freezing whenever I saw the deer raise his head from feeding. I was so intent on my movements and on the deer that I didn't see my long shadow poking way out to my right. Suddenly the buck came to attention. I took two quick steps to give me the clearance I'd need for a good shot, but the

It's important to watch where your shadow falls as you stalk mule deer. You can bet the deer will notice.

buck was gone. I stared at the spot he'd been watching to find out what had spooked him, and there was my great, long shadow reaching out across the landscape in the low angle of sunlight.

Sunrise and sunset are times to sit tight for deer. The shadow you cast at this time of day may be ten to fifteen times taller than you are. It really does appear like a giant moving across the terrain, and that is going to send any muley off into the hinterlands.

Even when the sun is down, you should avoid moving across any backlit landscape. Stay off ridges and hilltops where your figure may not cast a shadow but where it will stand out clearly in silhouette.

So it's the little things that count. That's what the light and dark of mule deer hunting comes down to in the end: re-membering to take off or put on your hat, looking in the right direction, knowing what the sun is doing to your shadow, putting your watch in your pocket to prevent it flashing in bright sunlight. Any of these little details can make or break a mule deer hunt.

STILL-HUNTING

I often hunt on a rise of land called Heartbreak Hill. It gains about 800 feet in elevation in little more than a third of a mile, a pitch that discourages a fair number of hunters. I like it for that reason. But usually I wheeze and pant up the slope, with little attention to hunting, until I reach less precipitous terrain.

One day last fall, however, a fresh snow combined with a cold snap made me approach the climb with a bit more finesse. Conditions seemed right for mule deer to be seeking warmth anywhere across the southwestern slope, so I took the hill one slow step at a time with long pauses in between. It's a pace that has prompted friends to comment, "Curtis must be after snails again."

It is a slow pace, I must admit. Well over an hour after I'd started, I was just approaching a little knob where I knew the topography would give me some relief. It was there that a large patch of hair brought me to a standstill. The midsection of a muley standing between two large fir trees less than fifty feet away is enough to give a rush of buck fever to any hunter. And it did to me, but still I did not budge.

The tag in my pocket was for a buck, and both ends of the beast before me were hidden behind tree trunks. I moved nothing but my heart and my eyeballs for what seemed like hours—perhaps five minutes. Fifteen years ago, I would have inched two feet to the left for a look at the deer's head. Instead, I stood like a statue.

The mule deer moved forward an inch at a time; it was probably just getting out of bed, still half asleep. It might have been a doe with others bedded over the rise where I couldn't see them, but I was betting on a lone buck. So when the deer's nose finally poked into view, I wasn't surprised to see the antlers that followed. Aiming carefully and without hurry at the deer's neck, I fired. And the buck dropped in his bed.

The pattern of that hunt represents my most successful mule deer tactic for the past decade. Slow and careful stalking has gotten me within sight of mule deer without spooking them. Then statue-like patience has allowed me to take clean shots at stationary targets of my choosing. In essence, this is still-hunting because even though you aren't always standing still, your moves are made in a way that minimizes the *detection* of movement.

Still-hunting has the advantages, without the disadvantages, of both stand hunting and stalking. When standing, you greatly decrease your chances of being detected by game because you make no movement. You can concentrate on looking for game instead of looking where you are going, but of course you are also limited to one field of vision. While stalking, you cover a lot of ground, increasing your chances of seeing game and affording a change in scenery. You are physically involved in the hunt, but deer also have an easier time seeing your movement.

Mule deer see movement much better than they identify stationary objects. If you're caught out in the open while still-hunting remain still instead of dashing for cover.

Deer depend largely on the motion of things to locate and identify them by sight. Although the structure of their eyes gives them excellent vision forward, sideways, and even back along their flanks, it is the movement of objects that alerts them to danger. On numerous occasions, in a variety of situations, I have stood quietly in the presence of deer that—without scenting me—have behaved as though I were just another pine tree or huckleberry bush.

So the key to the slow-motion hunting tactic is giving the appearance of standing still even when you aren't. This requires coordination, balance, and muscle control. Think of it as a series of motionless standstills connected by a series of fluid steps. The steps should be graceful. Jerky movement is a giveaway. Continuous movement is a giveaway.

Watching my cat has given me some good pointers on the art of still-hunting. Underhouse (the name is a long story) weighs sixteen pounds and sometimes sits embedded in the rug before the fire like a furbearing boulder, unmoved, unmoving, immobile. To look at that great heap of slothfulness, you'd never guess he is a superb stalker of wildlife. But at work outside, and under the house, he is the epitome of fluidity. Head straight, body low to the ground, eyes glued to his prey, Underhouse slides across the terrain like some noiseless, fuzzy pull-toy on unseen wheels. So far, his rewards for such apparently motionless movement have been voles, weasels, rabbits, shrews, mice, squirrels, and a vast assortment of birds. I will not be surprised when he drags home the neighbor's dog.

What his tactics have taught me is this: Know where you are going to place each step before you take it. Watch the terrain for game as you make your move. Move with your legs, not your arms and torso. Move like a slow-flowing stream. Glide to a standstill. Be systematic about scanning your surroundings for game. Look with your eyes, not your head or your body.

Still-hunting is sort of a slow-motion ballet, and although I have never taken ballet lessons, I have no doubt they would help perfect stalking techniques. Some professional football players practice ballet to gain the same benefits: strength, stamina, balance, and grace.

Ballet lessons aside, you have to be in good shape to still-hunt. The fluid movements and the statuary stances require muscle control and coordination. It's a lot more than a slow walk in the woods. After you've put in four or five hours of this kind of hunting, don't be surprised if you're worn out.

The technique requires concentration, too. You have to be in constant touch with the terrain and with the possible presence of game. You can't hunt well if you're preoccupied with paying for Judy's braces or worrying about the fight you had with your boss.

I remember a morning I tried to hunt for mule deer when I had a number of things on my mind—an important appointment in the afternoon, a flat tire to be fixed, several business contacts to make, a friend of a friend arriving that night for dinner. As I tried to concentrate on my surroundings, bits and pieces of these other matters kept crowding into my head. Within an hour and a half I'd spooked a buck, several does, and who knows how many more deer I hadn't seen. So I simply called it a day with barely two hours in the woods.

The next morning, with all the distractions attended to, I had the feeling I could move through the woods like the fog. And I came home with a nice muley.

The amount of time you spend actually standing in this method of hunting depends on several factors. At a minimum, I'd say you should be at a standstill about half the time. At particularly good vantage points in the terrain, you might stand still for half an hour or more, especially in the morning and evening when game is likely to be on the move. I have also remained at a standstill in the middle of the day at places where game might be bedded.

In one place where I often hunt there is a stretch of hawthorn flanked by a hillside where I can see down into the brush. I have spent the better part of a morning taking five minutes to move fifteen or twenty yards and then standing for twenty minutes to examine the cover below. On one such occasion, I'd been at a standstill for close to half an hour when two big muley bucks arose from their beds almost directly below me. I could have easily walked right on past if I'd been going at a more conventional hunting pace.

Hunting at a standstill can be particularly effective during the rut, as an experience I once had illustrates. Late in the afternoon toward the end of the season I was doing my snail routine across an open area on a sparsely forested hillside when a hint of movement on the ridgeline made me stop. It might have been wind in the branches of the fir trees, so I watched for repeated movement in that same spot. A flicker appeared in the trees farther up the ridge, and then a doe stepped into the edge of the clearing. She looked right toward me as I stood there like a stump in the open. For the next fifteen minutes, I watched five more does come over the ridge and move slowly along the tree line.

Earlier in the season I might have moved on at this point, but I had a feeling a buck might be at the end of the parade. And one finally did appear, head low and neck outstretched in the typical courting stance. Because of my stump-like appearance, none of those deer recognized me for what I was. And I was able to take slow, steady aim at the buck I wanted.

Of course, the temptation at times like these—when you're caught out in the open with game coming into view—is

Hunting with an extra dose of patience during the rut will often reveal a fine buck trailing a group of does. (Rodney Schlecht)

to take those few extra steps to get behind a nearby tree or bush. But you'll do well to resist the temptation. If a deer has taken note of you as an object on the landscape—much as it would note a stump or boulder—the sudden disappearance of that object will make the animal very nervous. Even if your presence hasn't been noticed, movement of any kind on your part—once you have made visual contact with game close at hand—is movement that begs for detection. Immobility is by far your best cover.

Although still-hunting is a particularly good tactic when you are hunting alone for mule deer, it doesn't have to be limited to solo hunters. It is possible for two or more hunters to sweep an area for game by moving abreast and within sight of at least one of the others. The key here is to prearrange your pace and the length of your standstills. But it adds another element of concern in that you not only have to concentrate on where you're stepping as you scan for game; you also have to keep synchronized with the other members of your party.

Clearly, still-hunting does not cover much territory. You might move just a mile in three hours. So you have to be hunting in an area where you can expect game to be. That doesn't mean something is going to be there every time you hunt, but you have to *hunt* as if something is going to be there. The temptation to hurry through perfectly good deer habitat on a hunch makes sense only when the hunch is backed up by specific conditions (weather, hunting pressure, time of day) that

When done properly, still-hunting is a deadly tactic. This hunter jumped this buck while it was bedded on a side hill. (Bill McRae)

can be expected to have a definite influence on the where-abouts of game.

Once, while I was hunting mule deer early in the season before snow covered the ground, even my most careful move-ments couldn't prevent the occasional snap of a twig or the crunch of dried balsam root. I didn't make a noise with each step, but every five minutes or so I'd step on something that would sound off, giving me the feeling that anything within half a mile had heard it.

Figuring that my hunting would prove fruitless, I de-cided to hurry up the hill and hit a wood road where I knew the going would be quieter. About twenty yards into a fast, noisy walk, I jumped a buck that was up and away through the trees before I even thought to raise my rifle. To this day I think I could have gotten that deer if I'd only kept "moving at a standstill."

By far the most defeating element in this method of hunt-ing is the sudden feeling that you may be pussyfooting through an expanse of forest devoid of deer. The bucks are over the ridge or down in the hollow, you'll suddenly decide, and that thought quickens the step, disrupts the concentration, and to-tally ruins the hunting tactic. Let's face it: There will be days when you act like a cat about to pounce in terrain that holds nothing but jeering squirrels and crows that caw at your antics. But still-hunting only works if you think and act as if a huge buck will appear any instant. And if you concentrate on what you're doing, you will certainly improve your chances of that happening.

HOW MULE DEER FIND YOU

Not long ago, I talked with a young wildlife biologist who had spent one opening day of deer season sitting on a knoll above some brushy coulees in New Mexico. He figured it would be a good way to get a sense of what the mule deer and the hunters were up to. His observations were revealing.

"I saw more bucks than hunters, and their combined movements looked like a lopsided game of chess. The deer were obviously the experts. They outmaneuvered the hunters all morning long. The whole time I sat up there, I didn't hear a shot fired," he said.

The story is undoubtedly a familiar one, for the acute senses of smell, hearing, and vision possessed by the mule deer usually give them a distinct advantage in their attempts to avoid hunters. Knowing how, when, and where to locate deer does you little good unless you also know how, when, and where *they* can locate *you*. Only then will you be able to consistently find muleys before they become departing blurs on the landscape.

SENSE OF SMELL

Of all a deer's senses, its sense of smell is the most acute. Research suggests that in a breeze of ten to fifteen miles per hour, with the temperature and humidity in the fifties or sixties, a deer can catch your scent up to half a mile away. That means you're going to have to work at minimizing these ideal conditions in order to have any chance of making contact with a muley.

Air movement is probably the first thing we think of when hunting. The old adage of staying up or cross wind to your game is a time-tested basic rule, but keeping your scent from reaching the nose of that big buck is a bit more complex than staying on the proper side of the wind. Here's a look at air currents and how deer react to them. It might just change the way you hunt.

Thermal winds originate locally as a result of differences in air temperature. Warm air rises; cold air falls. So local breezes tend to blow up hills during the day, then flow back down hills and into valleys when the temperatures cool as the sun goes down.

Where there are no hills, these wind shifts will occur in the lowest parts of the landscape, the lakes, ponds, and even swamps. Breezes will flow away from them during the day and toward them at night.

Almost every aspect of a mule deer's daily routine—bedding, moving, feeding—is influenced by these air movements. Just watch the deer. They feed and move into the wind, nosing the air for danger ahead and eyeing their back trail for danger behind.

What this means in relation to their routines is that deer tend to move to higher ground in the early morning when the thermals are still flowing downhill but are about to change. This way, when a deer beds down at a higher elevation and the wind shifts to an upward flow, the scent of any predator following its fresh trail will be carried up to the deer.

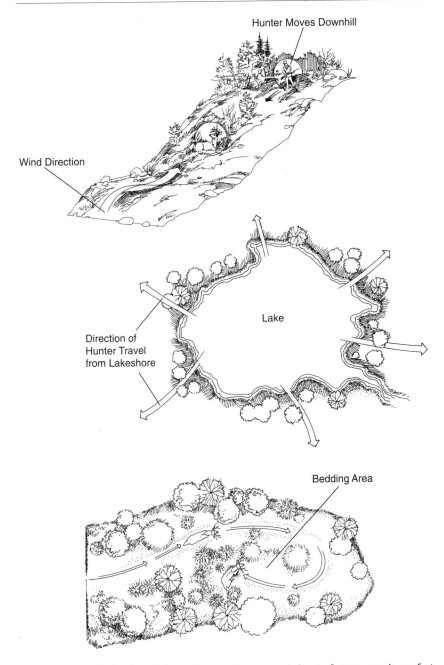

Hunting downhill [top] or inland from a lake or pond [center] puts you in perfect position to move down or in on deer once the wind shifts. During prevailing or storm winds, expect deer to walk in a loop before bedding down [bottom].

Conversely, toward evening, a deer will head down to feeding grounds at lower elevations while the wind is still coming uphill so it can nose the air for danger ahead. But the wind direction will soon switch, and again the deer will get the scent of any predator trying to sneak up its back trail.

Where game trails are involved, you'll find mule deer using only the trails that give them this kind of wind advantage.

To turn this to your advantage in hilly country, you'll want to be up high in the morning, just before the air switches from downhill to uphill. In flat country, near bodies of water, you should be farther inland. Then, once the deer are bedded down, you can move down on them without being scented and probably without being seen, since they tend to bed facing the wind.

But local winds are sometimes overridden by prevailing winds or by storm winds that don't allow local morning and evening wind reversals to take place. When this happens, deer use a clever ploy to keep the wind in their favor. They still head into the wind when moving to their bed—although this may be in a different place than usual—but just before bedding down, a deer will make a loop downwind for fifty to seventy-five yards so that the wind will be coming from its back trail, providing an early warning system while it's at rest.

Knowing this clever habit, you can use fresh track patterns to determine a deer's bedding site. As long as the tracks lead into the wind, keep following them. But as soon as the tracks turn away from the wind, it's a sign that the deer is bedded a short distance ahead of you and in the same direction the tracks turn.

Once you've identified a likely bedding area, move to where the tracks turn downwind and wait. Your scent will soon reach the bedded deer, and he will make his move. But you will be waiting for that.

Although a moderate breeze is favorable to deer, a strong wind is not. It creates a confusion of scents in the air, and deer have a difficult time separating various odors. This makes them nervous and sends them in search of protection from the wind.

Several years ago while hunting some forested slopes in the Rockies, a weather front came in and kicked up a wind that turned the forest into a perpetual motion of leaves, branches, and tree trunks. Shortly after the wind came up, two does appeared, nervously bobbing and weaving like two boxers. It looked as if they thought they'd gotten a whiff of me, but they weren't sure.

Instead of giving up on the hunting, which was my first reaction to the wind, I decided to see how the does would continue to react to the weather. In the course of two hours, I followed them up a series of draws, over a saddle, and into a thick stand of firs on the lee side of the divide. The deer were constantly on the move and extremely jumpy, but they were never able to confirm my presence.

Within the protection of the fir trees, everything changed. The wind died down to a whisper. The deer stopped their fidgeting, and I became a recognizable presence. At the same time the does became aware of me, I caught a fleeting glimpse of a buck leaving his bed at the top of the sheltered slope. Evidently, I'd located a favorite sanctuary from the wind.

No longer do I stay at home when the wind is high. In mule deer country, I head for pockets of thick forest on protected slopes. This windy-day tactic has produced a respectable number of successful hunts.

Moisture is another subtle, weather-related influence on a mule deer's ability to catch your scent. Because odors are gasses that are most clearly detectable to animals when combined with moisture, a deer's moist nose is extremely effective at interpreting scents on the air. Low humidity, however, tends to dry out nasal membranes, reducing a deer's ability to smell.

Ironically, moisture can work in your favor when it comes in the form of precipitation. Falling mist, rain, and snow act as a screen to odors, and also carry them to the ground.

One opening day when I was anxious to get into the woods, I left home well before hunting hours opened. By the time I'd hiked through a light rain to the edge of the forest, it was still too early to hunt, and I settled down on a log to wait. As rain dripped off the bill of my hat, I wondered if it wouldn't make more sense to be home in bed, but I waited until hunting was legal and then walked over a rise and into a grove of aspen. There, a mule deer buck and I surprised one another, and my deer hunting ended for the season.

The buck couldn't have been more than 100 yards from me while I sat on the log. A light breeze was reasonably favorable for him to pick up my scent, but my coming over the rise was a complete surprise to his nose. I can only assume that the rain had dampened my odor enough to offer me that sporting opportunity.

HEARING

Hearing is a mule deer's second line of defense against danger. I have only to consider the familiar sight of a muley facing me, his big ears looking like great cupped sonar receivers, to be reminded of the acuteness of their hearing. Deer are selective in their interpretation of noises, though. Habitual sounds are acceptable. It's the foreign noise that puts a deer immediately on the alert.

Sitting with my back against a ridge-side fir, I once watched a big muley buck walking calmly to the sounds of a squirrel scuffling in the leaves, a crow cawing overhead, and a broken branch scraping on a tree trunk. But when my foot snapped a twig as I tried to improve my shooting position, the buck bounded off in an instant.

These bucks, still in late-summer velvet, are using their sonar-like ears to help identify potential danger.

This is not to say that deer can't become used to man-made noises. Deer consistently feed along highways to the sound of nearby traffic. And I have to laugh when I think of the times I have avoided hunting in areas where timbering was going on because I thought the noise of the chain saws and logging trucks would disturb the deer. I finally talked with some loggers who chuckled at my belief. They said they always got deer during the first few days of the season. The deer became so used to the logging noises during the summer that it didn't seem to bother them at all.

This same acclimatization to manmade noise seems to hold true with rifle fire as the hunting season progresses. Even early in the season and at close range, the sound of a gunshot won't necessarily frighten a deer. The duration of the noise is so short that it is difficult for deer to locate. Consequently, they often hold their ground while trying to place the sound instead of taking the chance of blundering into what is making it.

Once, as a novice hunter with a bad case of buck fever, I ran into a group of six mule deer—five does and one forkhorn. Before I finally zeroed in on the buck, I had fired five shots in half as many minutes. Yet none of the deer bolted. They just milled around in the same general area, trying to figure out where the shots were coming from.

Although I don't recommend the practice of missing your first shot, I have learned that you may have a chance at another shot if you do miss. So don't go stomping about after missing your mark. It will probably be your movement, not the sound of the shot, that will spook the deer.

SIGHT

A mule deer's vision, in most instances, seems to be used to verify what smell and hearing have already detected. And although a deer's sight is excellent, it has some drawbacks. Mule deer see a world devoid of color. Consequently, hunter orange is not the eye-catching splash of color humans see in the woods. Instead, it's a patch of gray that may, nevertheless, look unnatural in surroundings that are naturally dappled.

For this reason, you should try to break up your silhouette by taking advantage of bushes, trees, and rocks. Avoid ridgetops, especially in open country where your entire outline, not just your hunter's vest, will stick out clearly against the horizon.

Another quirk in a mule deer's vision (which I touched on in the last chapter) is that its eyes are designed to detect moving objects, but they have a difficult time recognizing stationary things.

An incident occurred last hunting season that has been replayed dozens of times in my hunting career and that typifies a mule deer's reaction to stationary hunters. I'd been moving very slowly along a hawthorn-filled draw in muley country when I spotted a young buck about the same time that he became aware of something wrong in his world. Both of us stopped still in our tracks, but the buck's curiosity or nervousness, or both, finally got the best of him. Taking a few tentative steps, he strained his head to one side and then the other, all the time looking directly at me. His nose tested the air, and he

Mule deer have an excellent range of vision—roughly 310 degrees—but they primarily use sight to confirm what their noses and ears have already told them.

slowly began to circle downwind of my position. Then the deer exploded into the brush with a snort that seemed intended to clear my foreign scent from his nostrils. Had I been interested in bagging the buck, I certainly would have had plenty of time, for he seemed to be looking right through me until his nose helped identify what I was.

When I first started hunting, I'd always try to conceal myself when I sensed I was being looked at by a deer. I figured once I was out of sight—assuming it hadn't heard or smelled me—the deer would no longer be nervous. This tactic never worked. I'd move behind a tree, ridge, or rock, and inevitably the deer would get even more upset and disappear. I can only assume that these deer were more comfortable with my presence (even though they couldn't identify exactly what I was) than they were with my sudden disappearance.

Certainly, any movement on your part is more obvious to a deer than you think it is. I've tried with little success to move closer to deer when they appeared to have their heads diverted or when I was under the cover of low light. However, researchers have discovered that a deer can take in about 310 degrees of its surroundings because of the curvature and the bulge of their eyes. And they have extremely good night vision.

Finally, research has established that muleys have a fairly small home range. In studies of mountain-foothill habitat in western Montana, for instance, the average summer range of a doe mule deer is only a little over half a square mile. The average summer range of a buck before rut is less than 2½ square miles. On the open plains, of course, these ranges are much larger.

It is clear that mule deer are intimately familiar with their home territory. They know their surroundings the way you know your backyard or your front sidewalk. When something is out of place or when something foreign comes on the scene, their senses pick up on it immediately. Only by knowing how these senses operate can you tip the odds in your favor.

MOVE WITH THE FLOW

While hunting mule deer I occasionally get the feeling I once got in Spain when I was a young man. I was standing beneath a blunt sun in the main square of a provincial town. Not another soul was out in that heat, but I could feel a population of eyes remarking on my presence from the cool shadows behind doorways and windows. Come evening, however, I went completely unnoticed by these same locals as they ate and chatted and drank, filling with activity the same square where I had stood out earlier that day.

Mule deer, like the local residents of any area, have a definite rhythm to their lives, and that rhythm is defined by when and how they eat, rest, travel, and bed. Even social pressure influences the ebb and flow of their activities. When as a hunter you are out of step with that rhythm, you are as noticeable to deer in the woods as I was in the Spanish square at siesta time.

This suggests, of course, that we can identify a certain flow to the shenanigans of mule deer. And we can. Consider how they eat.

The timing of mule deer meals is influenced as much by their need to ruminate as by their hunger. Because they must take the time to chew their cuds in the process of digesting food, they must rest between frequent feeding periods. And especially in the fall, feeding periods occur day and night.

Typically, daytime rumination breaks come early and late in the morning and early and late in the afternoon. Muleys usually choose to ruminate during the day right in or near their feeding grounds. A deer will simply lie in a sweet bed of pine needles or walk into the tracery of nearby branches and lie down to chew its cud and take in the surrounding scenery. The only sound it expects to hear is the munching of its own cud, and that chewing stops if it senses the intrusion of foreign noises.

Even the low rustle of balsam root or the soft snap of fir twigs caused by your approach puts the deer on instant alert. Your movement will not be mistaken for the sounds of other deer because all the other deer are quietly ruminating also. In this situation, you are as vulnerable to early detection by mule deer as you'll ever be while hunting them. The solution, of course, is to sit out these rest periods along with the deer. When they stop, you stop. When they move, you move.

A deer on the move is not an ethereal spirit. Granted, it is a lot less clumsy than you or me, but it doesn't put its feet on the ground in total silence. And it has four feet to worry about. Mule deer brush against bushes and tread on twigs. They tear off snowberry leaves and cedar branches; they rip up bluegrass and silktassel. And when they're doing all this they can hear the little snaps and crunches made by their neighbors, who are doing the same thing.

Your snaps and crunches can blend in with the deer's, provided you keep them at the same intensity and pace, and provided you move in the same direction as the deer.

Mule deer usually bed down to ruminate (chew their cud) after they feed.

Feeding muleys move about randomly. They take a step and nip the end of a wild rose, then they look up and, chewing, move a few feet to the low-hung leaves of a serviceberry. Out of sight, just behind a slight rise in the damp forest floor, I have heard the slight ticks and whispers of their feeding movements. And I have moved into sight of the deer with my own soft sounds mistaken, I assume, for the snaps and swishes of other feeding deer.

This feeding activity is not only random, it occurs mainly off-trail. Game trails may cut through the heart of mule deer feeding grounds, but deer rarely just stand in the middle of a trail to fill their bellies. They move off-trail to reach the best forbs, berries, and fruit. And they don't move nose-to-tail like a string of packhorses. They scatter over a broad area munching and moving, munching and moving.

As long as you don't crack a big stick or get tangled up with a wrong-way wind, feeding time is a good time to move in on mule deer from an off-trail position. They are distracted. They are making their own noise. And you can blend in.

Exactly where mule deer feed depends on local food preferences and the availability of choice edibles. Local lore and some judicious scouting will point you in the right direction.

But as a rule of thumb, north slopes provide the best food during the fall hunting season. Here, summer plant growth is the most delayed, meaning that vegetation is frequently still succulent long after food on sunnier exposures has dried out. In addition, north-slope moisture provides thicker cover that shields understory plants from killing frosts.

Another reason muleys choose north slopes for feeding during the day is that they offer more protective cover than most other places. At night, however, darkness provides sufficient cover for muleys to travel anywhere. After nightfall, they often move down to more open areas, especially in agricultural regions where crop leftovers offer nutritious pickings that deer hesitate to go after during the day.

As a result, major daily movement for muleys is downslope in the evening and upslope at dawn. You can think of it as their daily commute, and you don't want to be caught bucking the traffic, so to speak.

Like commuters, deer tend to use specific travel routes to get to and from daytime and nighttime activity centers. So their movement occurs on trails, in a definite direction, and at a let's-get-there pace. This doesn't mean they break the speed limit, but they do walk at a purposeful pace that is unlike the random meandering of a feeding deer.

This is a movement you should try to fall in with. I know some hunters who sprint up hills and ridges in the pitch dark so that they can be hunting down on deer at first light. But deer moving uphill at this time are very alert to what's going on

Knowing when mule deer will be feeding, bedding down, or on the move allows hunters a greater range of opportunities to cross paths with a buck.

ahead of them, and this puts these well-meaning, if somewhat overzealous, hunters at a distinct disadvantage.

You should time your downhill movement for the hour before sunset when the deer are coming down or in daylight during muley feeding times. You should make your uphill trek during the hour or so after first shooting light.

Whether you're going uphill or down, you should travel on established game trails along with the commuting muleys. Don't go off scuffling around in the bushes. Off-trail sounds and movements are particularly disturbing to mule deer at these times.

Now, I know what you are thinking. If I'm going in the same direction and at the same pace as the deer, how am I going to catch up with them? Well, like commuter traffic, all kinds of feeder trails connect with main trails that lead to and from daytime and nighttime feeding and bedding areas. So deer traffic funnels in from these trails like traffic on the entrance ramps of L.A. freeways. And the best way to spot deer moving in from side trails unobserved is by going in the same direction they are.

Going with the natural flow of mule deer movement and inactivity is largely a matter of timing, and good timing is tied to the careful observation of mule deer activities in the specific area you want to hunt. Hunting deer has as much to do with watching deer as anything else. You have to know when the local deer go on the move and when they hole up. You have to watch how weather and hunting pressure influence the timing, direction, and location of their comings and goings.

If you're really in tune with all this, you'll be able to feel when the rhythm of your hunting movements is out of sync with the game you hunt. When this happens, you should know enough to get out of the square at siesta time.

REPETITION FOR BIG BUCKS

A lf Twiller's approach to hunting mule deer is boring. He hunts the same patch of ground every day, day in and day out. He follows the same route on every hunt, and he hunts at the same time every day. He's slow; he's methodical. In a word, he's a bore.

But he brings home trophy bucks with yawning regularity.

Alf is fond of telling me, over and over, that the secret to getting a big buck is repetition. By hunting the same ground continuously throughout the season, you dramatically increase your chances of bagging a trophy. You get to know the terrain intimately, including where to walk, where to look, and how to look. You also have the advantage of closely monitoring changes in deer movement and behavior. And you increase your odds of being in exactly the same place as a muley.

Of course, you have to apply this system to the terrain that big mule deer bucks are apt to use in the first place, and that may not be where you're inclined to think it is.

Wherever you see many deer congregating, there are probably only does, fawns, and young bucks. Mature bucks will be off by themselves (alone and in groups) except during the rut. The terrain they choose for themselves is usually on the fringe of what we think of as good mule deer habitat. Although does and fawns gather where forage is plentiful and diverse, bucks often hang out where the land is not as productive.

In mountainous habitats this often means ground close to the timberline. Alpine meadows with clumps of subalpine fir are favorite spots for muley bucks before the snows set in. There, they can find plenty to eat without moving far, and the islands of fir are easy for them to fade into if danger approaches.

At the other extreme, bucks also like forest fringes close to open lowlands. Brushy margins of agricultural land near forested hills are usually thought of as a whitetail's domain, but muley bucks hide there, too.

Once you get into the prairies, bucks are usually found on the periphery of hardwood draws. While does and fawns occupy the heart of the gullies where cover and food are in greatest supply, bucks are out on the edges.

Muley bucks occupy similar fringes in the breaks along major rivers. Instead of heading for the deep mazes of eroded landscape closest to the river, they move into the shallower drainage heads with less cover.

In all cases, trophy bucks hang out where most hunters don't expect to find them or where hunters are unwilling to go. It is in these marginal areas that you should look for the signs of big bucks. This is important, because you may not see the buck himself until after you've hunted an area for quite a while.

Alf tells the story of repeatedly hunting near a sidehill seep and seeing deer tracks in its muddy edges that made his eyes bulge. He hunted the area all that season and saw the huge tracks imprinted anew every three to five days, but he didn't spot the buck until the last week of the season when he caught a glimpse of its mammoth rack.

Alf persisted in his tactic of repetition, and by the middle of the following season he pulled up in my driveway with the trophy buck in the back of his truck.

Tracks are likely to be the most obvious indication of the presence of a big buck. They will show up in snow, moist earth, dust, and sand. A trophy-sized buck will have tracks that measure 3¼ to 3¾ inches long. (While it is difficult to tell the difference between the tracks of mule deer and whitetails, understanding the habitat you're hunting should clue you in.)

Areas where bucks are making fresh rubs should be incorporated into your "hunting loop." (Rodney Schlecht)

Rubs are another sign that bucks are in the area. Made as a scent and sight sign for other bucks and for does in the weeks leading up to rut, a rub is made on a sapling that is usually three to four inches in diameter. Larger, more dominant bucks make a lot more rubs than younger bucks, so where you come across numerous fresh rubs you should settle down to do lots of repetitious hunting.

The relative age of a rub is easy to determine by the sap that has bled from the exposed wood. When the sap is still sticky and runny, it has been made within the last few days. Older rubs contain sap that has filmed over but is still soft. Very old rubs have sap that is hard and crystallized.

Once you've settled on a spot that shows the signs of a good-sized buck, you should decide on an appropriate hunting route. This may take a little scouting. You might want to hunt the area two or three times before you choose the one route you're willing to stick with.

After I'd finally decided to take Alf Twiller's advice, I ran into a big clump of mountain maple that had been thrashed so badly it was almost dead. It seemed like the perfect spot to focus on, so I designed a hunting route that went pretty much all over the terrain surrounding the maple rub.

I had hunted the route for several days before I realized that there was an unobtrusive little draw that angled uphill from one edge of my pathway. On a hunch, I decided to include the draw in my hunting circuit. Ten days later I found the big rub-maker bedded in the top of that draw. Since then I've carefully checked out all possibilities in the area before settling on my final route.

Of course, the route should pass any spots where you've located frequent signs of a big buck, including tracks, rubs, and beds. Bucks will frequently freshen rubs, and beds—or at least bedding sites—are often reused.

Make a route that covers a variety of terrain. Go down ridges and across the tops of draws. Traverse hillsides and skirt terraces in otherwise steep areas. Move around to different aspects—south slopes, north slopes, east slopes, west slopes. Include a lot of diversity in the landscape you explore and stop often to glass the surrounding country.

Don't pass up patches of cover, but try to tailor your route so you hunt above them and can look down into them for any indication of a buck in hiding.

Be sure your route passes a variety of forage types: grasses, forbs, sedges, woody shrubs and bushes, and trees such as aspen. And if there's water nearby, include it on your route. Look for creeks, springs, or ponds where there are signs of deer use.

Don't think of your hunting route as a means of getting somewhere, because then it tends to become a fairly straight line from point A to point B. A good hunting route to use over and over will be quite circuitous, curving around and circling back, going up and down, across and over.

Design the route so that it takes three or four hours to hunt very slowly—from legal hunting light to around 10 A.M. Muley bucks are most active in the morning, so this is the time to hunt unless you have spotted a big buck showing himself regularly at some other time of day.

One of the reasons younger bucks survive to be big bucks is because they get to know their territory intimately. And one of the reasons for using repetition as a hunting tactic is so *you* can get to know that same territory as well as the buck does.

If you are a veteran whitetail hunter, it may seem as though all this repetition would alert any buck in the area to the pattern of your movements and help him avoid you. But, ironically, what it seems to do instead in muley country is acclimate deer to your presence and make them less wary. After all, you come through the area every day at the same time, following the same route. You move slowly and quietly, without causing any trouble. A deer can get used to that, up to a point.

A big buck is not suddenly going to stand out in the open after you've passed by every day for a week, but he also won't leave the area for one that's hunted less. Instinct tells him he's better off on turf he knows well than on unfamiliar terrain.

Remember, time is in your favor. While the buck gets used to your presence, you get to know more and more about where he lives. You start by learning where to walk. On the first few trips over your finalized route, do a little trail grooming. Move bothersome sticks and branches out of your path; brush noisy leaves away. You may want to fine-tune your route to minimize noise by skirting around spots that are particularly difficult to travel because of downfalls or other obstacles. As you get to know your route, you will find that you spend less time looking at the ground trying to decide where to put your feet and more time looking for the buck.

I remember being surprised by the way a friend of mine hunted the first time I took him over a route I'd traveled numerous times before. Letting George go first, I could see that

Bucks like this one are easier to spot when you are already familiar with every detail of a specific area of cover. (Rodney Schlecht)

he kept checking out the ground and missing parts of the terrain that might have revealed a buck. George is a careful and successful hunter, but he had to concentrate on things that repetition had taught me to do instinctively.

As you spend more time hunting the same route, not only will you be able to walk it more easily, but you'll also learn more about where to look for deer—and where not to look. We've all spent long minutes staring at a bush that looks like antlers or a stump that resembles a deer's rump. These are distractions that you can ignore once you know them well and can recognize them for what they are. Instead, you can focus your attention on "windows of opportunity" into the surrounding vegetation and topography. You will only discover these windows by hunting the same route over and over and recognizing those places where you can stand just so and see into the heart of the hawthorn thicket or down a hallway of trees to a secluded huckleberry patch. This is the kind of "learned looking" that gives you the edge over other hunters and over the buck.

Not only do you learn where to look, but you get to know *how* to look. As you reach the top of a certain rise, for example, you may find that you should look first to the right and uphill if you want to get the jump on a buck that may be standing in an opening you can see through a narrow slot in the bushes. In other places, you'll learn to stand and carefully scan the curtain of vegetation for signs of a buck—a thickening in the density of the cover, or a curved line where everything else is angular.

While repetition hones your ability to know where and how to walk and look, it also alerts you to changes in deer behavior and movement. Changes in bedding and feeding sites due to weather conditions are probably the most important factors to pick up on by noticing shifts in the concentration of tracks and droppings. These can help you focus your attention on certain areas of your hunting circuit under certain conditions.

Recently, a light snow cover showed a fairly uniform spread of tracks made by a buck using an area I was repeatedly hunting. But after a heavy snowfall and cold winds, all the tracks became concentrated around a steep draw that my route covered. By hunting that section of my circuit particularly hard over the next two days, I ended up with a very big buck.

When Alf Twiller saw it, he smiled from ear to ear and simply said, "Repetition gets results."

HUNTING SPOOKED MULE DEER

We've all spooked a lot of mule deer, and when we do, we usually mutter some malediction and consider the deer gone. If there's snow on the ground, we may follow the tracks. But when the ground is bare, we tend to give little thought to exactly where and how far a spooked muley will move. Consequently, we may come home empty-handed when we could have come home with a buck had we just known a few facts about how a spooked muley behaves.

When a mule deer bolts, it often uses both vegetation and topography for escape. It may go over a ridge or behind a hill rather than move into nearby timber or brush.

As I've noted earlier, given a chance, muleys will move uphill, and they often choose a route strewn with obstacles—rocks, downed timber, or low brush. Their use of the stott, the four-legged bounce characteristic of a spooked muley, is designed to get them uphill and over obstacles efficiently. When they depart this way it gives you the impression that the deer will run forever, when in fact it's usually just the most expedient manner of getting over the next ridge. So don't try to predict the distance a mule deer will run by the gait he uses to get there. The deer that slinks off behind some bush may move just as far as the one that stotts out of sight.

Once a deer has been spooked it will continue to look back in the direction of whatever it was that startled it. If the deer sees you in pursuit, it is likely to move faster and farther than it would have had you simply stayed put until it was out of sight. Besides, you will have a better chance of determining the deer's direction and whereabouts if you watch its departure without moving. It may disappear behind trees or bushes only to reappear again farther up a hill or along a ridge. In addition, the muley may stop to see if you are following, giving you a chance at a good shot.

Mule deer do not necessarily associate the sound of a rifle with danger, although they may be startled by it. If you fire and miss, don't assume that your target is headed for the next county. Do assume that a deer's spookiness will be heightened if it has recently been frightened.

When a spooked mule deer launches into its famous four-legged stotting gait, clearing a fence is child's play.

Since a hunter's movement and scent are more disturbing to a muley than a gunshot, pursuing a spooked mule deer requires some subtlety. Start by using still-hunting tactics, if you haven't been using them already. Move under the cover of vegetation or topography. Don't use the same path the deer has taken, since it will tend to look back in that direction, and remember to keep the wind in your favor.

HUNTING HIGH COUNTRY

Because mule deer bucks are often found high in hilly terrain, you may often find yourself hunting ridges close to divides. This is good escape country for deer. They have the option of disappearing over side ridges or over the top of the divide itself. Despite those choices, I have found that muleys have a preference for going over the side ridge that is nearest to them and farthest away from you. Once in a great while, a deer I've spooked in the bottom of a draw will cross over the same ridge I'm on, but that is uncommon. Muleys also seem reluctant to top over the divide itself, unless that route is unquestionably the shortest way to put a ridgeline between them and you or unless there is thick timber up there and vegetation is sparse over the next ridge. *You* may not know these facts about what lies over which ridge, but you can be sure the deer will.

In order to cover the two most likely muley escape routes in this high-country hunting situation, head directly up to the divide and follow it to the side ridge beyond where you spooked the deer. If there is timber on the other side of the divide, you may want to still-hunt into it for 75 to 100 yards. But return to the divide at the point where it is intersected by the side ridge the deer may have used for escape. The canyon or draw on the other side of that ridge is the most likely place to find the spooked deer, and approaching it from above is the best tactic, since the muley will be more concerned with looking back in the direction from which he has come. Several years ago, while using this tactic, I was able to down a large four-point buck I'd spooked ten minutes earlier because he was intent on looking at his backtrack and not at me.

HUNTING LOW COUNTRY

The terrain in the transition zone between croplands and forested hills is another haunt for muley bucks. They are masters at blending in with low sagebrush and tall grass. But when they are spooked, they head for the hills. You'll rarely find them running up open hillsides or even timbered ridges. Instead, they invariably seek the safety of brush and timber high up in the bottoms of canyons and draws. This gives them the options of two side ridges and possibly a divide to hide behind if further flight seems necessary.

Approaching a spooked muley in this case is a matter of the big climb. Hike up whichever of the two adjoining draws that will put the wind in your favor. If the draw isn't too long, go all the way to the top before you cross over and start working down the draw the muley entered. If it's a long draw or canyon, don't go more than about ¼ mile before looking into the muley's draw. I like to peek over the ridge and check it out every 100 yards or so, and if it's sparsely vegetated, I continue on up

A buck that simply trots away from something it can't identify probably isn't spooked yet. (Rodney Schlecht)

beyond the ¼-mile mark until I'm above good vegetative cover. Then I cross over and work down in a zigzag manner.

HUNTING UPHILL

Hunting uphill is not the best tactic for going after mule deer. They have a habit of looking downhill, and air currents have a habit of wafting scents uphill. The combination puts you at a distinct disadvantage. You have to get up the hill before you can hunt down it, though, so you might as well spend that up-hill climb hunting.

Frankly, I've gotten a fair number of muleys that appeared above me as I worked my way uphill—but I've spooked a lot more. Their response is predictable: they head away from you uphill, but they know you are still down there somewhere even after they've moved out of sight. That almost always prompts them to head over a ridge if one is nearby.

Which ridge they choose will be anybody's guess, although muley bucks try to keep the wind blowing from the direction in which they came, if that's possible. It usually isn't, so you should continue moving up the draw in which you spooked the deer until you are about ¼ mile above where you first saw it. Then check out each adjoining draw. Choose the draw with the most cover and work down that one first, but don't go down below the elevation where the deer spooked. If that draw turns up nothing, climb back up and work the other draw in the same manner.

There is no easy way to follow a spooked muley in this situation. But while searching for deer often means a great deal of legwork, the effort *can* pay off. On one occasion, after pushing a king-sized buck up a draw I was hunting, I spent an hour working out the adjoining canyon I thought he'd gone into. He wasn't there. It took me another half-hour of huffing to get back up the draw to work out the other canyon. Two hours after I'd spooked the buck, when I was beginning to think he was long gone over the top of the divide, I came down on him feeding quietly in some huckleberries.

HUNTING DOWNHILL

Whenever possible, hunt mule deer by coming down on them. You'll spook far fewer deer this way. Those you do spook will probably head downhill first, but that's not their favorite move. It won't be long before they come circling around to some uphill terrain, typically one of the two side ridges. Your choices here are the same as in the uphill hunting situation, but you have the advantage of being above the deer to begin with.

Hunting downhill helped this hunter get within range of a trophy. Always keep the wind either in your face or coming from the side. If the wind starts coming from behind you, the deer below you will scent you and spook long before you even see them. (Bill McRae)

It's possible to intercept the path of a spooked muley simply by moving laterally to one of the adjoining draws. Choosing the right draw is, again, a matter of assessing the wind direction, considering the cover offered, and perhaps even drawing on hunches and instinct. None of these will assure your success, but they'll get you a lot closer to success than considering a spooked mule deer to be a lost cause.

MAP OUT YOUR MULE DEER HUNT

The hunt began in a 727 as it came in low over the mountains on its approach to the local airport. I sat in a window seat checking landmarks and looking for the canyon where I live. Suddenly it opened up below me, the familiar ridges and draws I'd hunted for years and the knob way back along the divide where I always turned around and headed home.

But beyond the knob, perhaps revealed by a slight deviation in the plane's usual flight pattern, I got a glimpse of a secluded saddle, a hidden quirk in the landscape, something I never knew was there. It was enough to set my deer-hunting wheels in motion.

On the way home from the airport, I stopped in town at my favorite sporting goods store.

"A map of Cougar Creek," I said. Jerry smiled at my request. "You, my friend, are in luck! I just got in a bunch of those 7.5-minute topographic maps. Bet it's got your house on it. Maybe you can even see in the windows."

Jerry exaggerated just a tad, but the map did have my house on it. Every square mile around the house took up a 2⅝-inch square on the map. Compare that with the 15-minute topo maps most of us grew up with (on those maps one mile takes up only one inch), and the details shown on the 7.5-minute series will make your head spin.

At home I bent over the map for a good hour, getting a new perspective on the landscape I thought I knew so well. I was surprised by the hidden draws, bowls, and hillside benches I found on the map, which I had never discovered in fifteen years of bushwhacking the same country.

The 7.5-minute maps, in fact, give a perspective on the landscape that is impossible to gain in the field. On the ground, your sense of the lay of the land is obscured by the topography itself and the forests that cover it. But looking at these maps is like hanging over the terrain in a helicopter.

Topo maps in the 7.5 series can improve your mule deer hunting in unfamiliar country as well as in terrain you think you know well. Used properly, they can show you hidden areas of good mule deer habitat and the easiest ways to get to them. They can show you where hunting pressure is likely to be heavy and where muleys are probably going to move to avoid it.

On the Cougar Creek map, the saddle beyond my "turn-around" knob was represented clearly by the contour lines. I decided then and there that the saddle would be the site of my first mule deer hunt of the season. It would be my first "mapped-out" hunt.

Using a topographic map is easy once you get the hang of it. At the heart of reading a topo are its contour lines, thin brown lines that indicate the presence of hills, valleys, saddles, and ridges. Each contour line represents an imaginary line on

MAPPING YOUR MULE DEER STRATEGY

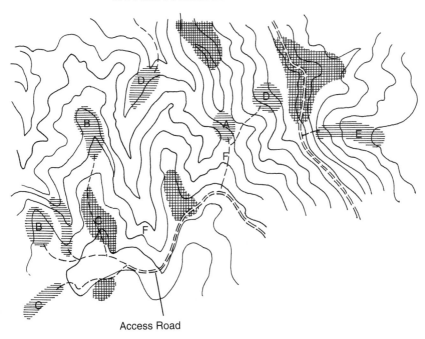

Access Road

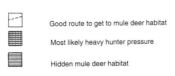

Good route to get to mule deer habitat

Most likely heavy hunter pressure

Hidden mule deer habitat

A Saddles are natural crossover points for muleys escaping heavy hunting pressure. Look for a saddle with at least one side that is not easily accessed, and post up there at the beginning of the season.

B Terraces or benches along steep ridges offer mule deer a level resting place with a view of their surroundings. From here they can see and smell danger. These features are most productive in remote areas that receive little hunting pressure.

C Because moisture collects in draws and ravines, these areas attract mule deer with a wider variety of edible plant life than the surrounding slopes and ridges. Hunt draws in the mornings and late afternoons, when deer are likely to be feeding.

D Gentle topography surrounded by steep terrain, whether it comes in the form of draw, a ridge, a bowl, or a hill, offers muleys a protected place where they can easily move around. Use your map to find the easiest way into such areas.

E Ridges that run east and west are choice hunting spots when it is especially cold and snowy. Mule deer will spend the night on the north slope, where the vegetation is thicker; during the day they will sun on the open south face. Hunt the ridgeline at dawn and dusk, and you can catch muleys crossing from side to the other.

F Routes into good pockets of muley habitat can be found on a topo map, and deer themselves often make trails into these spots. Ridgelines and ravine bottoms are the usual routes, but also check out contour lines indicating easy paths that sidehill along steep stretches of terrain without gaining or losing much elevation. And don't ignore the long way around.

109

the ground where every point is the same elevation. It's as if a huge lake has risen to that particular height on the landscape, and its shoreline, represented by a single contour line, follows the ins and outs of the surrounding terrain.

The distance between contour lines is called the contour interval. My Cougar Creek map has a contour interval of forty feet, which means every time I move up or down one contour line on the map, it's the same as gaining or losing forty feet in elevation on the ground. It's as if the imaginary lake has risen or fallen forty feet. The closer the contour lines are on the map, the steeper the terrain is on the ground.

Where contour lines nose or bulge out toward higher elevations, they represent a draw. Where they nose or bulge toward lower elevations, they represent a ridge. Hilltops are shown by small circular contour lines. Streams and drainages are shown by blue lines. Forested land is green; open land is white.

After a little practice reading one of these maps, you'll begin to get a very clear picture of the landscape it represents, even if you've never set foot on it before.

The actual process of mapping out a mule deer hunt in any area starts with avoiding the places that will get a lot of hunting pressure. Usually terrain within a half-mile of roads is going to get trampled pretty heavily by numerous hunters, especially in draws, along ridges, and on gentle slopes. It's certainly possible to get deer in these areas, but they will be jumpy. There will be a preponderance of does and fawns, and the bucks will tend to move away from all the commotion.

So, as a general rule, start checking your map for likely mule deer hotspots beyond a half-mile buffer zone surrounding mapped roads—even logging roads if they're known to get much traffic.

Identifying places on a map where mule deer are likely to congregate requires some consideration of their basic needs: feeding areas, bedding areas, sheltered areas, and (maybe most important during hunting season) escape areas.

Before they're going to feel very comfortable eating and resting, muleys are going to want to feel safe. That's why the secluded saddle I'd seen from the airplane sent me running for a map. The map revealed what I suspected. The saddle came at a point along the divide where the east drainage had easy access by road but where the west drainage could be reached only by hunters willing to walk some distance on foot.

Come opening day, I suspected quite a few muleys on the east side of the saddle would head for that natural crossover, the only one for many miles in either direction, in order to get into some country where hunting pressure was light.

My main concern was that the saddle would be a favorite spot for hunters who regularly hunted that east drainage. But while scouting it out before the season, I found that a side ridge blocked a view of the saddle from the road. On opening morning there was only one other hunter in the saddle, a guy who smiled wanly and said he wondered how long it would be before someone else found the place. A Cougar Creek map stuck out of his pocket.

I told him how I'd found the spot and swore myself to secrecy. He admitted that he'd taken bucks three seasons in a row by just sitting by the game trail that crossed the saddle. Within four days both of us had filled our tags. So for starters, check your map for saddles, and hunt them at the beginning of the season.

Benches are also good places for mule deer. When I think of the places I've found the most mule deer beds and where I've found the most muleys in their beds, I have to think of benches or terraces along otherwise steep ridges. Muleys like to rest on level ground with a view of their surroundings. A terrace or bench allows them to look for danger and smell trouble rising on air currents before an intruder actually arrives.

Not just any bench will do, however. Mule deer are going to look for a quiet bench with little hunting pressure, and that's what you should look for on your map. Remember, what you see in the field can be very deceiving.

For years I went back and forth to hunt deer on a gravel road running next to a steep ridge that flattened out briefly and then tipped sharply down again. That niche in the landscape intrigued me, but the apparent effort required to get there kept it out of reach until I checked it out on a map. Out of sight, on the backside of the ridge where the bench wasn't even noticeable, a logging road ended. With a stiff but short walk, I found I could be hunting a spot that from all appearances in the field was too much of a hump to handle. Since then I have taken two big bucks from that bench; both of them were in their beds.

Bucks that are interested in food are going to leave their beds and head for draws. These are the spots where increased moisture

Carefully studying topo maps and scouting out likely habitat may lead you right to a muley hangout.

offers a wider variety of edible plant life than the surrounding slopes and ridges, so draws are good places to hunt in the mornings and late afternoons, when deer are likely to be feeding.

Whenever I'm walking or driving in mule deer country and I see a steep draw that makes me say "no way," I check it out carefully on a 7.5-series map. Often the map confirms my initial reaction by showing contour lines packed closely together all the way to the head of the draw or ravine, but occasionally my map shows a draw that starts out very steep at the bottom and then eases off towards the top.

There's a draw like this along one of the most heavily traveled muley hunting access roads in my county. The bottom of the draw ends within 100 yards of the road. Hundreds of hunters pass it every week of the season, but because it heads up out of the canyon floor with the trajectory of a rocket, it's totally ignored by hunters.

A close look at a map, however, shows that the top third of the draw is quite gentle until it nears the divide, where it angles up sharply again. By following a side ridge off the divide, I can be in the gentle section of this draw within half an hour of leaving my vehicle. I've never seen another hunter there, but I've come across lots of muleys.

This sort of gentle terrain surrounded by steep terrain is something to look for on your map whether it comes in the form of a draw, a ridge, a bowl, or a hill. Most hunters don't want to fight what looks like difficult terrain. Muleys sense that and gravitate towards places that are easy to move around in but look hard to reach.

Under at least one condition, however, muleys will congregate in places that look difficult even on a map but which are fairly easy to hunt. When it's especially cold and snowy, mule deer move to ridges that run east and west. They spend nights on the north slope of the ridge where thick timber offers overhead cover that slows radiant heat loss, and they spend days on the south slope where sunshine warms them. The travel time between the two slopes is a short hop over the backbone of the ridge.

The contour lines on both sides of a ridge may appear close together, but the backbone itself is usually plenty wide for easy walking. By hunting these ridgelines at dawn and dusk when the weather gets really cold, you can catch muleys crossing over.

This trophy 4×4 was taken off a side ridge in the rolling mountains near Buffalo, Wyoming. (Jay Cassell)

With any of these mapped-out hideaways for hunting mule deer, it's important to locate relatively easy access routes to reach them. Ridgelines and ravine bottoms are definitely places to check out on your map, but don't overlook those all-important contour lines. It's often possible to sidehill along a steep stretch of terrain, not gaining or losing much elevation, in order to get into a good pocket of muley habitat. The deer themselves often make trails into these spots, and these can make access surprisingly easy, even along steep ridges and bowls.

Finally, don't ignore the long way around. Easy access doesn't necessarily have to be short. Take a careful look at your map. One good-looking pocket of mule deer terrain that I mapped out went unhunted for two years because it looked too difficult to get into. Then, on a winter evening when I was perusing maps before the fire, I started following contour lines *out* of the pocket. One of them intersected a ridge about three quarters of a mile away. The next summer I pioneered a route from the trail into the secluded mule deer hideaway. It was a half-hour hike, mainly on game trails. In the fall, that mapped-out hunt produced a dandy buck.

Mule Deer Habitat

MULEYS AMONG
THE TREES

The vast forests of the West cover much of the prime mule deer habitat in this country. Roughly half the mule deer population in the U.S. lives among the trees. There was a time when I thought this meant a walk in any Western forest would turn up a muley and that mule deer hunting in the timber would mean certain success. The summer I moved to Montana, all this seemed possible. But that was almost thirty-five years ago.

I arrived that August somewhat in awe of the huge expanses of forested land, but refusing intimidation, I spent most of my free time hiking into the timbered foothills on scouting forays for the upcoming hunting season. There was not, to be sure, a muley behind every tree trunk, but there were lots of deer. And with my expectations for fruitful hunting confirmed, I entered the big-game season as green as the needles on the trees beneath which I hunted.

I continued to see deer, probably the same plentiful does and fawns I saw in August and September, but not the big bucks I had dreamed about. Not the big bucks I had *not* seen, but whose nearby presence I had assumed.

It wasn't until the middle of the season that I saw my first buck—a young forkhorn that I took with a sense of urgency and bewilderment. But there had to be more than does, fawns, and forkhorns in those huge tracts of timber.

I know now that the mature bucks are there in the trees along with all the other deer. But they are only in *some* areas of the forest, and those places change throughout the season and throughout the day. I know now too that hunting muleys among the trees is something quite different from what I'd imagined that first summer I scouted the forests of the West.

Among the many things I did not know back then is something I have since stumbled upon through experience, which the Montana Department of Fish, Wildlife, and Parks has confirmed through research. Come the opening of almost any big-game season, it's the does and fawns that occupy the large middle elevation of forest, which constitutes the major portion of timbered mule deer habitat. The bucks are on the fringes of this range—down in sparse timber near croplands and up near timberline next to alpine meadows. They are in these locations because here they can avoid competition with the does and fawns for both food and cover.

It isn't until the first snows of the season that some of those mature bucks start to drift down to the middle elevations, and it isn't until rut that the lower bucks move up. By the end of the season, this combination of snow and rut have usually pushed and pulled most of the deer into a belt that may be only 700 to 800 feet wide, just above their winter range.

Ironically, it is these *un*forested winter ranges that are the first keys to knowing where to hunt in the timber. These ranges will be open south- and west-facing slopes on mountain foothills where sage and bitterbrush grow. They're typically located between 5,000 and 7,000 feet. And it's the belt of timber directly above these areas that hosts the growing concentrations of mule deer as the season progresses.

Dave Pac is a game biologist who has spent years studying mule deer in the mountain forests of the Rockies, and who sees many hunters ignoring the importance of this stratified concentration of deer.

"What a lot of people do is hike right through that belt where all the deer are. It will be 7:30 in the morning, and they're already at the upper level of the belt, and these guys start thinking: I'm going to keep bucking all the way up through the snow on this ridge, I know there's a big buck camped out in the deep snow somewhere. And there might be, but most of them are going to be down below."

Hunting muleys among the trees is more than keying in on

these areas above their winter range, however. I think back, again, to my greener years. As a Connecticut Yankee coming to the West, I was used to the rolling hardwood forests of New England where to know the woods on one side of a hill was to know the woods on the other side.

Hunters who understand how and why muley bucks move within mountain habitat will have the greatest success.

121

I learned that forests are different in the West.

That first year in Montana, I spent the tail end of the season hunting with a young native I'd met. He'd take me to some of his favorite hunting spots, and I figured I could learn some things about mule deer hunting among the trees if I just kept a sharp eye on the kinds of places he selected.

What I learned was puzzling. Every place we went seemed to have a south- or west-facing slope with a fairly open forest canopy. Although we saw plenty of deer, and even though I was able to fill my B tag with a nice four-point muley, I couldn't figure out why Wes never left those south and west slopes. I never asked him why because I didn't want to appear dumb. But I suspected there might be a gigantic buck on the other side of those hills we hunted.

One day toward the end of the season, I went by myself to one of those areas and worked up over the south slope to the other side of the divide. The north side of the divide was a different world. A dense stand of subalpine fir formed a thick canopy that made a twilight world out of the forest below. Through the gloom I could see logjams of deadfalls, and my visibility was less than 100 feet because of the density of the tree trunks. It was a difficult place to hunt, and a perfect place for deer to hide. I hiked back over the hill to the southern slopes.

All such north or east slopes in Western timber are not as imposing, but the additional moisture found in these areas does produce thicker stands of timber, which provide ideal resting and escape cover for mule deer. They are areas that deer move into, especially during the day, but they're also areas in which muleys move around very little. I decided I was not yet ready to hunt north-slope timber.

The south and west slopes, on the other hand, are where the deer go to feed—usually in early morning and late evening—and feeding means moving. This deer movement (in addition to the better visibility offered by the sparse forest vegetation) makes these locations much easier to hunt.

Looked at this way, those vast mule deer forests begin to get a little more manageable. Winter ranges clue you into the general areas to look for deer after they leave the fringes of the forest, and then keying in on south and east slopes helps narrow your hunting area even further. These are the places where the deer will often be. Seeing them there is another matter.

The forest, under all but the most ideal conditions, is a difficult place to hunt. You're likely to make noise while walking through the dried vegetation that covers the forest floor. Visibility is limited by the forest itself, and distinguishing deer amid the profusion of brush, branches, and tree trunks is an acquired skill.

The noise factor is most frustrating before snow arrives to help muffle sound. Under dry conditions, I've learned to look for fencelines—especially where cattle or horses have been grazing—to decrease my chances of making noise. Next to a fence, there is usually a path of sorts made by livestock and by people checking the condition of their fence. Fences in forested Western mule deer habitat usually mark the boundary between private lands and national forest lands. And these often occur at elevations that coincide with deer concentrations during hunting season.

Abandoned wood roads offer other quiet routes to use in hunting dry forests. These old roads tend to be overgrown, so they offer some cover for you. But their ruts are still fairly clear of forest debris, giving you a quiet place to walk.

The use of game trails is another possible way to avoid sounding like a steamroller in a potato chip factory when hunting in dry periods. As a matter of fact, one hunting circuit I have developed follows fencelines, wood roads, and game trails to take me in a mile-long circle that covers about 600 feet in elevation. Without the use of these pathways the muleys would hear me coming from hundreds of yards away during dry times in the season.

Moisture dampens sound, whether it comes in the form of rain or snow. A good rain takes the crunch out of dried leaves and grasses and allows you the freedom to stray from the beaten path. Snow is even better when it is fresh and dry, but it can be the worst of curses when it is wet and then freezes into a crust.

After I'd been in Montana for a number of years, a friend from the East came to hunt muleys with me for a week during the middle of the season. On our first day out, I suggested we sweep a broad terrace on a south slope where I'd been successful the year before. I showed Jim the start of an old fire trail and told him to follow it like the proverbial tortoise until he reached the clearing, where I'd meet him in several hours.

I had barely begun to hunt a parallel fenceline fifty yards from Jim when several does and a two-point came trotting over from his direction. Farther on, more deer crossed through the trees ahead of me, all coming from Jim's direction. I learned on reaching the clearing that Jim had been there for half an hour, and he hadn't seen one of the deer he moved out.

Clearly, timber is the place for still-hunting—that fluid, snail-like movement through the trees that requires concentration and all the grace you can muster. Timber hunting is no place for the heavy of foot.

I'm reminded of the time I helped guide a party of four men from the Midwest. One of them was a hulking fellow, as nice a guy as you'd ever want to meet, but a disaster among the trees. He cracked twigs and snapped branches with every step he took. We finally suggested that he take a stand in the area his companions would be hunting. Only then did he get a deer.

But even a slow and quiet hunter is going to miss seeing deer if he doesn't learn to systematically scan the trees for those telltale shapes and colors that suggest deer instead of twigs and tree trunks. Deer in timber aren't going to appear as whole objects. They're going to show themselves in bits and pieces—a leg, an antler, an ear—and that's what you should learn to look for.

A final consideration when hunting muleys among the trees is to use the topography within the forest to your advantage. Mule deer are very much in tune with the ups and downs of their terrain, and they use it for escape and for surveying their surroundings while resting.

As I noted earlier, muleys invariably head uphill when spooked, and they usually select a route littered with down-

Bucks like this one fall to hunters who learn to move quietly over natural pathways in the forest. (Rodney Schlecht)

falls. Both the exertion of moving uphill and the obstructions in the line of travel will slow down any predator pursuing the deer from below. For a hunter moving below, it usually means a fleeting glimpse of a muley's rump as it disappears uphill. When hunting from above, however, even a spooked deer may present itself broadside to you as it moves up through the timer to escape.

In addition, when selecting a place to rest, a mule deer will often pick a shelf or terrace on the upper portion of a ridge. From there he can watch the forest below and catch foreign smells carried on the rising daytime thermals. Your chances of spotting such a deer before it detects you are much better if you are hunting down the ridge from above.

But what, when all things are considered, are the ideal conditions for hunting mule deer among the trees? I recently posed that question to Dave Pac, who has spent more time observing muleys in the last twenty-five years than even the most avid mule deer hunter could in a lifetime.

"What I like to do if I have my choice," he said, "is go out during the middle of the week. Stay away from the weekends; take a day off. Pick a time when there's a good snowstorm one day and hopefully it's going to clear during the night and turn cold.

"Then get out there well before light, and at least be at the lower level of that belt where the deer are. And then, once it turns light, just move really slow and stick to the open canopy side of the ridge. Move through that, so you only cover a couple of hundred yards in an hour. Just let those deer move into you. That's the time of day and season when they're all going to be moving after the storm. They're going to be on that side of the ridge, and they're just going to be moving all over the place."

HUNTING THE LAY
OF THE LAND

A patch of ground I sometimes hunt for mule deer is an area considerably smaller than two square miles, located in the foothills of the Rockies. Despite its limited size, it offers a diversity of topography. There are draws and ridges, flatlands and steep hillsides. At one place or another these quirks of the landscape face every direction of the compass. The different features populate the terrain with a range of vegetation that runs from sagebrush knolls to thick fir forest and from grassland parks to lodgepole stands footed with huckleberry bushes.

Deer in this random chunk of land, which is typical of much of the mule deer habitat in the West, can find everything they need to make a decent living and have some comfort in the process. Consequently, it's a good place, an inviting place, to hunt muleys. And many people do hunt here, moving into the area from a variety of directions and methodically combing the ups and downs, the openings and the dog-hair timber, as if the deer could be found anywhere in the lay of the land.

Some hunters inadvertently run into luck; others never see a deer. For the most part, it's a game of chance. The hunters' odds are low, not because the deer aren't there, but because most of the hunters don't give enough thought to *exactly where* on that piece of land the deer will *choose* to be in order to satisfy their own needs.

The hunter who hopes to even the odds has to fine-tune his hunting location to the range of possibilities open to deer in that particular area at a given time under specific weather conditions.

To start the process of fine-tuning, the hunter must get to know the topography of the land on which he is going to hunt. By far, the best way to do this is to walk the terrain and cover all the nooks and crannies on foot. This doesn't have to be done during hunting season. In fact, it's best done either on summer mornings when wildflowers are out in force or in the edged air of early autumn afternoons. These are times when you can pay attention to the shapes and the slopes of the terrain and to what grows on it and where.

If this slow-and-easy process of learning the lay of the land is impossible, a topographic map of the area will suffice. Study it in your motel room after a dinner of cowboy steak and hash browns at the local eatery. Check out the contour lines and the compass bearings.

Then, before you start hunting, consider a deer's needs— food, shelter, water, escape cover, and a place to bed. And ask yourself: Where *in the lay of the land* are deer most likely to satisfy these needs, given the time of day and the weather conditions? The answers, you will find, are always changing, but they are always tied to the topography and what it has to offer.

Consider some of the most prominent topographic features of mule deer country.

North and east slopes grow the thickest timber. They also have the most shade and moisture, the thickest downfalls, and the thinnest understory.

This is just what I was looking for one warm Indian-summer afternoon in October after spending the morning hunting open timber. Frankly, I headed for the thick timber on that north slope more for my own comfort than anything else. The temperature must have been more than seventy degrees, and my long johns were a lot more than I needed in the direct sun. Besides, I hadn't seen a deer since midmorning.

The air under the thick cover of fir felt like the air in a dirt cellar, and it smelled of moldering deadfalls. A gray light washed around the tree trunks, and it took several minutes for my eyes to adjust.

In mountain/foothills habitat, mule deer often feed on south- and east-facing slopes early in the hunting season. (Rodney Schlecht)

I sat on a stump, enjoying the cool, damp air. Silently, a rump patch moved behind a tree. A dozen feet away, an ear flicked. Deer began to take shape. And suddenly, it seemed natural that the mule deer materializing before me would seek comfort from the heat in the same place I would. In fact, in any kind of weather—wind, cold, snow, even rain—muleys will look for relief in the same kind of cover you and I would. It's a convenient arrangement for a hunter.

North and east slopes aren't just hot-weather hideouts for mule deer, however. Look for deer on these slopes during low-temperature extremes, too. When it's very cold, thick timber acts as a shield against radiant heat loss. So you're likely to find muleys there on bitter days when the sun is down behind the hills or the horizon.

These same slopes, with their closely crowned trees, generally have less snow after a storm than the most sparsely timbered south and west slopes. Deer will move around on these north and east slopes when other areas are snowbound.

Finally, don't overlook north and east slopes when the hunting pressure is high. The thick timber and the downfalls make them difficult places to hunt. Consequently, many hunters avoid these slopes. Muleys sense this and move to this kind of topography in order to escape.

South and west slopes are the food producers. These slopes tend to be sunny and dry, and they grow moderate to sparse stands of timber interspersed with open parks. Understory growth in this kind of timber is good. So mule deer seek these areas when they want to eat.

These are the slopes I hunt on autumn mornings and evenings when the temperature seems to straddle the fence between winter and summer.

One morning at the end of October, I left the house early to reach one of my favorite south-facing foothills before sunup. It's an area that sees a good amount of hunting, but I figured I could be up in the hills before the big-breakfast bunch arrived. I'd hunt the southern exposures for feeding deer early on, then cross the ridge to the northern slopes when the forest got crowded. I counted on the deer to do the same thing.

Arriving at a sparsely timbered knoll, I glassed the long flanks of the south-sloping hills. In the open parks, frost had given the grasses a tin-colored hue, but nothing moved in the dawn chill. I watched the hillsides for a half-hour before moving up along a spine of timber that would get me mid-slope under cover.

Halfway up the hill, I could look across a large meadow and into the thin stand of lodgepole on the opposite side. That's where I found the deer. The frost had not been hard enough to hit the forage under the cover of those trees. Yet the trees weren't so thick that they inhibited good understory growth. In addition, the shade had retarded summer vegetation development enough so that some of the forage was still succulent and nutritious for the deer, even in October. However, most of the grass in the open areas had either been desiccated by the sun or freeze-dried by the frost.

Food is not the only thing that brings mule deer to south and west slopes; cold weather does, too. Although north and east slopes provide heat-loss protection when the sun is down, south and west slopes are the warmest places when the sun is up. Deer tend to gather on these slopes where openings offer full exposure to the sun.

Whatever direction a slope faces, it is seldom a flat plane. Its surface is usually wrinkled with ridges and draws, and these elements of the topography are important to muleys.

Ridges, even when they are covered with brush or timber, have more exposure than other parts of the landscape. Consequently, mule deer—particularly during hunting season—don't spend much time walking or feeding on them. The exception to this rule of thumb may come during the seasonal migration from high to low country, especially when it is a pressured move provoked by a sudden storm.

More frequently, mule deer use ridges as bedding places. You'll seldom find muleys on main ridges that make for the backbones of major divides. Their favorite bedding spots seem to be those unobtrusive side ridges that often get overlooked by hunters in a hurry.

These side ridges offer a number of advantages for a deer at rest. Although the exposure of a ridge puts deer at a disadvantage when they are moving or feeding, it works in their favor when they are bedded down. First, a ridge puts muleys on a point of high ground that offers them a good view of the surrounding topography. Also, sounds and smells can reach the deer's senses from both sides of the ridge, warning them of possible unseen dangers.

Because these ridgeline haunts are favorite places for muleys to chew their cuds, I often hunt this lay of the land during the middle of the day. In fact, last year I stopped to eat a sandwich at the top of a long side ridge on a chilly November day. It was a little after noon, and a spot of sun had warmed the rock I sat upon. The spot afforded me a good view of the countryside as I ate my lunch.

About 100 yards below me and just at the end of my line of sight, the edge of a small terrace broke the even descent of the ridge. My eyes kept coming back to that spot as I lingered in the drowsy warmth of the sun.

It wasn't until I'd shaken off the midday stupor and eased down the ridge another twenty-five yards that I made out the head and rack of a muley that was tucked into the huckleberry bushes in the middle of the terrace.

Of all the idiosyncrasies of mule deer terrain, draws, coulees, or gulches are probably the favorite places of the deer. The majority of the mule deer I've put in the freezer over the past thirty years have come out of this kind of topography. And there are good reasons for finding muleys there.

Draws tend to hold moisture, which fosters good forage growth for mule deer. Especially where the country is dry, draws will hold green vegetation long after the rest of the countryside has turned brown. This is a real drawing card for hungry muleys.

In addition to food, draws offer protection from extremes in the weather. They are cooler than the surrounding landscape when the temperature is warm, and they are warmer when cold winds rake the nearby ridges and hillsides.

There's a long steep-sided draw in the area where I frequently hunt mule deer. This cleavage in the north-facing hills

When the wind picks up, muley bucks will often seek out the shelter provided by deadfalls and heavier overstory cover on north-facing slopes. (Rodney Schlecht)

is known locally as "The Hole" because its upper reaches drop away so abruptly. In addition to being a local landmark, it is a local sanctuary for mule deer when the west wind is blowing in a storm or when it is just blowing for the sound of it, as is often the case in the West.

One day, I struggled with the wind on the west slopes just long enough to know that any sensible deer would be tucked into the lay of the land where it could find some relief. Then I headed for The Hole. The calm that prevailed at the bottom of that draw was somewhat unnerving, considering the force of the wind that wailed across its top. And the mule deer were in there by the dozens.

Despite the number of muleys I saw, the escape cover they were provided with in that confined area was extensive. As a matter of fact, most draws—in addition to offering food and shelter—have enough thick vegetation to give mule deer a pretty good sense of security.

The draw behind my house, for example, runs west-to-east. Its south side is dry and sparsely forested with old firs. The moist, north side was once thick with lodgepoles, but a recent infestation of mountain pine beetles has thinned the trees out, leaving both sides of the draw with fairly good visibility for anyone who hunts there. Yet the draw is a favorite of local mule deer. And one of the main reasons for this is the fact that the bottom of the draw has a rather extensive stand of aspen mixed with hawthorn. I can't count the times I have spooked muleys into this draw, only to have them disappear into the cover of these deciduous trees.

A final advantage for muleys using draws is that they can find several exit routes should they feel the need to escape. Uphill escape routes are favored by mule deer, and any draw gives them the choice of heading up either side or up the middle. Occasionally, they'll even surprise you and go out the bottom. It's no wonder muleys like to spend so much time in draws.

Despite the mule deer's tendency to stick to broken and uneven terrain, don't overlook flatlands when considering where deer are likely to find fulfillment for their needs. The primary flatland attraction for muleys is food. Whenever agri-

This mule deer buck was taken as it was using an escape route in a draw. (Jay Cassell)

cultural crops border wooded foothills, brushy draws, or breaks, mule deer are likely to use them as a convenient source of nourishment. The deer can come out into the fields to feed at dawn and dusk and during the night. Come daylight, though, they simply slip into nearby cover to bed down.

Once again, it's a situation in which the lay of the land provides the key to when and how muleys will use certain areas of their habitat to fill their needs.

SUMMIT MEETING
WITH MULE DEER

Wyoming's Wind River Range doesn't give way to its high country until you've hiked for several days. Trees finally become sparse and alpine tundra littered with glacial rock takes over. Summit Lake lies in the corner of an expanse of sedge, heather, and grasses. In the unobstructed rays of the late afternoon sun, it's the kind of place that makes you want to sprawl in the cushioning grass, close your eyes, and drift with the sound of bees. It's one of those sweet deceptions that can last for hours or merely minutes in the high country during the short summer.

It was late August. A chill creeping across the meadow reminded me of the equinoctial storms that could dump a foot of snow here at 10,000 feet within a matter of days. I sat up and pulled two big cutthroat trout from the cool grass. They'd be more than enough dinner for Glenn and me, I thought, as I started to rise. Then, slowly, I eased back to the ground.

The shadow I saw behind a clump of stunted fir might have been made by a bird or by a branch in the wind. But I was in no hurry to get back to camp. I waited. And it came again, this time coalescing into shoulders, neck, head, and the biggest four-point antler spread I'd ever seen on a mule deer.

My surprise was related as much to finding the deer at this elevation as it was to the size of the animal.

For fifteen minutes I watched it move across the meadow, flicking its ears and tail at flies, cropping forbs, and pausing occasionally to raise its big rack and survey the landscape. And what a landscape in which to find a muley! The stark rocky ridge behind the deer looked as if it had been snipped from tin.

Having marveled over the presence of the deer, I rose to go tell my fishing companion. The four-point, seeing me, merely meandered behind an island of weatherbeaten firs and resumed eating.

We saw the deer two more times before we left the high country—once early the next morning within 100 yards of where I saw him the first time, and again the following evening in roughly the same spot.

I was convinced that finding such a muley at that elevation had to be some kind of aberration. On the other hand, knowing the traditional nature of mule deer, I considered the possibility of coming back for the opening of big-game season. But it would be stupid to spend several days slogging into this high country much later in the year. If a storm caught me, I'd end up as freeze-dried groceries for the bears and mountain lions. Besides, there was no reason to think the deer would still be there.

"He'll probably follow us down the mountain tomorrow morning," I joked with Glenn the night before we left the high country.

I'd forgotten about the Wyoming buck by the next fall when I was fishing for small grayling that inhabit Emerald Lake in the

Bucks often utilize marginal alpine habitat in the high country before winter weather pushes them down.

Gallatin Range of Montana. The mountains were still free of snow, so I'd hiked in the 4½ miles for a final high-country fishing trip early in October. Early the next morning, as I crawled from my tent into the crisp air, I had a sudden reminder of the Wyoming high country. There, in a meadow silvered with frost, was another muley, another four-point, another surprise.

Quietly, I lit my backpacking stove, heated water, and sat back with a mug of sweet coffee and cream to watch the mountain mule deer. Like the Wyoming buck, he seemed secure in his movements as he fed casually on larkspur, columbine, and meadow rue. But as the sun broke over the peaks, he looked around the alpine bowl, then nosed his way into a clump of fir and disappeared. There he remained while I fished and pondered the phenomenon of high country muleys.

The bucks, it seemed to me, had to be using the high edges of the forest, just as they used the low forest edges, in order to avoid competition with the does, fawns, and yearlings for the food and cover of the forest heartland.

Hunting at these timberline elevations would certainly require some extra effort, and that's probably why I'd heard very little talk, at least in my section of the country, about going high for mule deer. Also, that's probably why the bucks weren't especially wary. They just didn't get that much hunting pressure.

Suddenly, the prospects of getting high on mule deer were looking more interesting.

Favorite alpine habitats, I'd learned from the bucks in Wyoming and Montana, seemed to have some common features. Both deer had been in timberline meadows above extensive forest cover. But the meadows had been dotted with small clumps of subalpine fir. The deer had selected locations with bowl-shaped contours where moisture seemed to remain throughout the summer. And that moisture nurtured plenty of forbs.

The bucks had also used these habitats in similar ways. The gray light of early morning and late evening appeared to be their time for feeding and moving about in the open. And the small, but often thick, islands of fir served as their bedding areas. They never seemed to drop down into more extensive forest cover.

During the entire time I had observed them, neither buck had moved very far from the spots where I'd first noticed them. They didn't have to. The very nature of their environment, with its remoteness and its severe topography, made them feel secure. In addition, there was plenty of forage within the relatively confined areas of the alpine bowls, and water was readily available.

When the bucks wanted to bed down, the clumps of stunted subalpine fir provided shade and cover. At these high elevations, the shady side of the fir islands might be fifteen to twenty degrees cooler than the sunny side. And for more protection, the bucks could tunnel into the middle of the vegetation, where they'd never be seen, even if you walked within a few feet of them.

In short, the deer had all their basic needs satisfied. And they could just hang out up there, fat and sassy, until the weather got messy.

All things considered, the situation for hunting bucks up high sounded ideal—with a couple of major glitches. The first was getting to the deer; the second was getting a deer out if I bagged one.

Back home, I started planning my hunt with a topo map of the local mountains. It seemed to make sense to choose an alpine location that was fairly close to an area I knew was an established mule deer winter range. So, using the maps, I located a drainage head that was about two air miles from one of these ranges, one with alpine meadows forming a natural timberline amphitheater. I also picked a spot that I figured I could hike to within an hour of the road's end.

I decided to use a timberline camp. If I didn't, I'd have to hike in the dark up there at daybreak, or I'd have to hike out in the dark if I got a buck in the evening. So on the opening day of rifle season, on a clear, crisp afternoon, I packed in a light camp and set it up below a hump of rocks at the base of the alpine amphitheater.

From the rock outcropping I could see for over a quarter of a mile in all directions above me. And that's where I went with my binoculars after dinner. The sun was putting on an extravagant orange and red lightshow over the distant mountains as I settled back against a rock to munch a candy bar and wait. And wait I did. But few waits have been more enjoyable, surrounded as I was with high mountain meadows, glacial rock, the whisper of the wind, and the occasional whistle of a marmot. It was an encompassing solitude that was uninterrupted until just before dark.

The noise might have been caused by the click of a hoof against stone or by loose rock on the nearby talus slope. But it pulled my eyes to a gray form halfway up the bowl. Through my glasses I could see it was a buck of substantial proportions, yet the light had turned the color of slate. I knew I'd have to wait until morning. And I counted on the deer bedding down in one of the clumps of fir.

It was still dark when I fumbled out of my sleeping bag and felt my way back up the pile of rocks. As light began to seep across the darkness, a chill rose up my legs and nestled into the small of my back, the reward for going without breakfast. But I continued to stare wide-eyed into the dawn, letting the islands of trees and the rocky outcroppings slowly take shape.

Against that backdrop, the buck came into focus close to 200 yards away. He moved at ease, a few steps at a time, stopping to crop food and then moving again, slightly uphill.

I am not a taker of long shots, which, in the low light, this appeared to be. However, the deer was getting farther away the longer I waited, and to move off the rocks in the open would have alerted him to my presence.

I aimed high behind the shoulders, and the concussion of the shot reverberated across the alpine bowl long after the buck was down and I was on my feet. It was a five-point including brow tines. I boned it after breakfast, and by 10 A.M. I was headed down on my first trip to the truck.

Since that morning, I have discovered a few more things about high-country mule deer. Perhaps most important is deciding whether the bucks are, in fact, likely to be up high. High-country hunting for muleys has to be keyed to their population densities. Natural fluctuations in deer numbers in any given area definitely influence the use of high elevations by bucks. When populations are at a peak, buck use of alpine areas is the greatest, but during population lows few deer may use these locations because suitable, uncrowded habitat is closer at hand.

Out of the typical ten-year span between population peaks, the peak year and the years just before and after it will offer the best opportunities for hunting high. Even during top population years, you have to keep a close eye on snow accumulation in the high country. Weather permitting, bucks will stay in the alpine areas until mid-November, but they may be long gone

It often pays to look for big bucks that abandon forest habitat for the safety and solitude of alpine country. (Rodney Schecht)

from these spots by the end of October if snow and cold hit early.

It's wise to keep a tally of the number and duration of fall snowstorms. If you figure the snow in the area you plan to hunt has reached a foot and a half, you're probably not going to find deer up there.

Although it seems reasonable to assume that bucks would leave the high country completely once the rut is underway, this is not always the case. Some bucks will drop down into the forest heartland during the night in order to chase the ladies, and then move back up into the alpine country to bed during the day. So don't rule out hunting high just because the rut has started.

Once you have decided that bucks are likely to be in the high country, there are a few logistical considerations to keep in mind.

When picking an alpine area to hunt, remember to key in on those closest to traditional winter ranges, but be realistic about how far you'll have to hike to get in *and* get out with your game.

Make your camp in an unobtrusive location close to an observation point that will afford you views of most of the alpine meadows above. High country hunting is one of those few situations where sitting and waiting for mule deer is the best tactic. The habitat is just too exposed and too rocky to allow much undetected movement. So use binoculars to glass the area in the early mornings and late evenings. And be prepared to make shots in the 250-yard range.

If for some reason you can't get a shot at a buck you've spotted, keep in mind that these bucks don't move around much. Chances are good that your buck will bed down within 100 yards of where you last saw him. Although you may not be able to pinpoint his location, you can do a fairly accurate job of narrowing down his whereabouts.

When you are forced to move in on a bedded deer, it's best to have one hunter do the moving, very slowly, while another stays put at a good vantage point.

When it comes to getting a buck out of the high country, I'd bone it completely. It will take you about an hour and a half if you've done it before. Then put the meat in cloth bags, unless it has cooled overnight, in which case plastic bags are all right to use. Lash the antlers upside down to your pack and decorate them with hunter-orange warning ribbons.

As a final perspective on high-country mule deer, consider this: When you're hunting at these elevations, you aren't going to see a lot of deer. But the deer you do see are probably going to be bucks. And the bucks are probably going to be big ones. So even if you only see one deer, chances are very good that it will be the buck you are looking for.

BACKYARD MULEYS

Every year deer hunters trudge past my house, cross the hay-field out back, and disappear into the lodgepole forest that begins at the base of the hill. Most of them head for the ridge that marks the divide between the canyon where I live in southwestern Montana and the next canyon to the east. From there they can hunt hundreds of square miles of national forest land that is prime mule deer habitat by anyone's standards. Yet every year a considerable number of those hunters return with their deer tags unfilled.

It's not that mule deer are scarce. Plenty of those hunters see bucks that they could bag. Yet the typical lament from these deep-woods hunters is consistently the same, except for the specific name of the distant location.

"Oh, I saw a big buck back on Blue Mountain, but I wasn't about to drag it all the way out from there. Too bad. It was a nice deer."

There are other hunters, of course, who don't see muleys. And some offer excuses like, "The woods were too noisy," or "They must still be in the high country." I suspect, however, that some of these hunters have a problem with the size of the territory. There is so much of it, and the expectation of seeing a deer in the next draw—and the next one after that—is so great that they hunt too fast. They miss seeing deer in their attempt to hunt as much territory as possible.

I'm well aware of these problems of hunting in big country, and I used to cope with them myself in similar ways.

My education in the ways of backyard mule deer all started one opening day. It was a cool, clear morning at the end of a week of dry weather. I had been scouting the woods several days earlier, and hard as I tried to walk quietly, each footfall sounded as if it were landing on a carpet of crunchy cereal. My only quiet option seemed to be in sticking to the wood road of a neighboring rancher. It wouldn't take me very far from the main canyon road and nearby houses, but it seemed my only choice.

At the top of the knoll in back of my house I paused to wait for legal daylight. Lights still shone from the houses below, and I wondered if I might not be better off having breakfast in one of those comfortable kitchens. There seemed small chance of seeing a muley so close to civilization. Nevertheless, I shouldered my rifle and strolled slowly along the wood road into the trees.

The buck seemed as surprised at my presence as I did at his. He lowered his head, and his steps became tentative.

Within an hour of leaving home, I was back by the fire having coffee. And the buck was hanging in the shed.

The incident was a fluke, of course. At least that's the way I saw it at the time. The buck had no doubt been a maverick, not yet spooked by hunting pressure. My hunting friends agreed.

However, my experience the next year suggested otherwise. I did very little muley hunting until the end of the season. As a matter of fact, the chances of finishing the year without getting a deer looked very good as I stepped out of the house on the last day of hunting season. The hour was past nine, and I knew three friends had already gone up the gulch behind the house. A shot had been fired earlier, and I was sure all the commotion had unsettled any deer in the vicinity.

But I kept remembering the backyard muley of the year before. There was no time to get deep into the woods. I'd have to concentrate on hunting nearby and hope for a repeat of the previous year.

Going directly up the steep nose of a side ridge that starts behind my vegetable garden, I gained several hundred feet in elevation before angling across to the head of a small draw. The draw is thick with timber—one of those places you have to hunt very slowly if you hope to see anything, much less get a shot off. The deep snow helped slow me down and effectively muffled the sound of any twigs I might have snapped below its surface.

At first I wasn't sure I'd seen a movement at all. But it was worth stopping to double check. Nothing more happened for several minutes. Then between one of the slits in the vertical world of trees, a horizontal patch appeared. An antlered head moved into another slit. I sat in the snow with my .30/06 readied until I saw the buck's shoulders.

Now I was beginning to wonder. Two backyard muleys in a row! One on the first day of the season, the other on the last.

A surprising number of nice mule deer bucks use thick brush and irrigation ditches near roads. (Rodney Schlecht)

One when there was no snow on the ground, the other when the snow was up to my knees. Maybe there really were such things as backyard muleys.

I certainly couldn't attribute their presence to the fact that they hadn't been spooked. There had been enough people hunting in the area that year to stir up a whole herd of deer. But neither could I claim that it was just the snow that had forced them so close to human habitation. The weather had been dry as a bone the year before.

I was contemplating these matters in my living room when the three hunters who'd set out before me came wearily back through my front yard. They stopped to say they had taken a shot at a mule deer heading up the gulch that morning. I said I'd heard the shot. It was the only deer they'd seen all day, and they'd gone miles back along the divide.

"You know, sometimes those muleys come down from the high country after dark," one of my friends started reasoning out loud. "They feed in the hay and wheatfields at night then just before dawn they head back to the cover of the deep woods. That one we missed was probably running a bit late."

"Well, Dave," I said, "he or one of his friends must have continued to run late because he's hanging in the shed right now."

There was a great deal of head shaking and soft muttering following my remark. I even began to feel a bit guilty. One of the guys had been out after a deer several times a week since the start of the season.

My friends attributed those first two backyard muleys to an uncommon turn of good fortune, but I was definitely beginning to believe otherwise. The next year's season made me a firm believer.

I purposely decided to spend my time hunting a limited area within about half a mile of the canyon road and its adjacent dwellings. My efforts were concentrated on the gulch out back. The first week of the season I went out three times. One time I saw no deer at all; twice I saw does. The fourth time I went out was the start of the second week of the season. At the top of the gulch, resting quietly in the sun, a three-point buck convinced me of the common existence of backyard mule deer.

There is nothing unique about the area I hunt. It could be any muley country where forest and agricultural land meet. Here, it is not at all unusual for muleys to stick to the periphery of pine forests, along the edges of fields and irrigation ditches within sight of roads and houses.

I'm convinced these backyard muleys are not seen by most hunters because they don't *expect* to see them. First of all, many hunters aren't yet looking for deer because they've just gotten off the road. Second, most hunters are moving too quickly and too noisily to see deer because they're in such a rush to get into "better hunting grounds."

Even when track concentrations indicate there are deer down low, along creeks, in fields, and at forest edges, many hunters believe they are the tracks of whitetails instead of mule deer. Even granting that this is sometimes the case, the whitetail assumption has led many a mule deer hunter past a prime buck.

Some skeptics will still balk, of course. Recently an acquaintance who heard me mention backyard muleys laughed at the idea of finding a good-sized buck so close to home.

"You may run into some young, inexperienced bucks that hang around close in," he said, "but it is no place to hunt if you're looking for a trophy."

I then related an incident that occurred before I believed in finding mule deer in the backyard.

Wally Hansen and I had been hunting up the canyon and back along the divide. We'd run into some tracks, and we'd seen some does, but not an antler had been visible. As a last hunch before returning home I told Wally I wanted to walk out on the nose of land that overlooks my neighbor's ranch house.

On the south side of the nose a thicket of hawthorn fills a narrow draw. It was late in the day, and I figured I might run into a buck emerging from the brush to feed. My attention was fixed on that southern thicket while I walked down the nose, but as I neared its end a movement to the north caught the corner of my eye. Wheeling around, I watched a six-point buck sneak out of sight. It was the biggest deer I'd ever missed.

The only place the buck could have been bedded was in a small brush patch of no more than a quarter-acre. It lay just above an irrigation ditch, beyond which stretched a plowed field, my neighbor's house, and the county road. Above the brush, open grassland rose a quarter of a mile before running into forest.

So much for the lack of backyard trophies.

But believing in backyard muleys and hunting them are two different things. Bagging a mule deer that is within sight of a road depends on knowing the areas where the deer hide and on hunting these areas thoroughly.

As the missed-buck incident points out, thick brush along irrigation ditches and creek bottoms is a prime location for muleys. These places are more often thought of as whitetail habitat, but muleys will also use them when they border the forested lands usually associated with mule deer territory.

These thicket areas are particularly difficult to hunt along, though. When you are outside the brush, you can't see into it, and when you're inside you can't see more than a few yards in any direction. Lone hunters will do best to post themselves in the late afternoon at a point where a sizable portion of the thicket's periphery can be observed. From such a vantage point, you are likely to see deer moving out of their cover to feed.

Thick timber bordering fields and other open land affords prime cover for backyard muleys. To hunt this type of habitat when there is no snow to cover the dry twigs and the grasses that tend to be such loud noisemakers, you'll be wise to stay on

Mule deer bucks will often inhabit areas near homes, fields, and roads. Finding them requires hunting thoroughly, quietly, and slowly. (Bill McRae)

paths, wood roads, or game trails. But a covering of eight to ten inches of snow will offer ideal conditions for hunting heavy timber. You can move more quietly through the heart of the timber, and you have a better chance of seeing deer against the light background of snow.

I prefer to hunt this kind of area alone. The theory that two or three hunters will push deer into one another may work when hunting more open terrain, but it doesn't work in thick timber. Any deer that is being driven by another hunter is likely to be on the run, and a deer running through thick timber is a blur—not much of a target.

I'd say the key to success here is to hunt by yourself and

to hunt very slowly. A silhouette is often your only clue to a deer's presence. It may be merely a hint of those mule-like ears or a subtle interruption in the color and pattern of trees. Many times I've had to use binoculars or my rifle scope to determine whether an object was a deer or just a figment of my imagination.

Finally, any draws or gulches located near open fields or close to roads and houses provide good backyard refuges for mule deer. Ideally, you'll work these potential hiding places by coming down from above. When you can't view the entire area and you are hunting alone, it's often smart to work the same gulch three different ways. Come down one shoulder of the gulch or draw, then go up the other shoulder, and finally come down the bottom of the gulch itself. To some people that may seem like beating a dead horse, but a quiet hunter can pass within a few dozen yards of an unseen deer without disturbing it, providing the wind is right. There have been times when I have not seen deer in a relatively confined area until my third pass through.

Backyard muleys do exist. Finding them requires that you hunt their likely hiding places thoroughly, quietly, and slowly. And hunting them

You'll rarely find bucks bedded down in the open like this when hunting near houses and roads, but if you are willing to work carefully through heavy cover you'll find deer that other hunters pass by in their rush to get up into the forests.

safely requires that you be completely familiar with the location of nearby buildings and livestock. But going after backyard bucks, in my estimation, is often more productive than hunting a seemingly limitless expanse of habitat.

BORDER CROSSINGS

By concentrating their activities at places where several plant communities border one another, mule deer can take advantage of the different food, shelter, and escape cover these areas have to offer. This gives deer the greatest diversity of habitat choices.

Their predilection for borders, and for frequently crossing back and forth between them, leads them to these specific places. You'll find mule deer on the borders where forests meet valley croplands and also at timberline where forests meet alpine meadows. You'll find them in elevational bands where one plant community gives way to another. And you'll find them within a plant community where islands of different vegetation occur.

Throughout the mule deer's range, these borders are often widely separated. But occasionally you'll find a number of different plant communities bordering one another within a very short distance. These areas are real muley hotspots.

Borders themselves are often gradual, with vegetation from both communities intermingling to create a band where plant life has more variety than in either community by itself. Aspen/conifer borders often blend together in this manner and are ideal places to hunt muleys.

Other borders are abrupt. In the Great Basin, foothills covered with piñon woodlands often give way quickly to sagebrush flats. The borders between forests and meadows are also often abrupt, reflecting the difference between well-drained and poorly-drained soils.

These abrupt tree-meadow borders are prime places for muleys. The unique combination of sun, shade, soil conditions, and moisture afforded by these particular borders fosters the growth of many plants that can't grow elsewhere. And studies have shown that the frequency of plant species and the amount of vegetation on the border between forest and meadow is twice as much as it is fifty yards out in the meadow itself. In addition, during the growing season, there are always some forage plants that are at their peak of stored nutrition and digestibility along this border. No wonder muleys gather there!

Of all the borders, the one most overlooked by hunters is the one between forest and valley cropland. We tend to associate mule deer with trees and hills, so we usually march right into a forest before thinking seriously about hunting these deer. That's a mistake.

Even fields that have been harvested have leftovers that attract muleys. They're suckers for cultivated edibles. And they can feed on the edge of a grain or alfalfa field while still having excellent cover and bedding sites in the bordering forest.

A band of brushy vegetation often intrudes between cropland and conifer forests to form a second border that we usually associate with whitetails. As detailed in the previous chap-

Areas where forests meet grasslands are mule deer magnets.

ter, many a muley buck grows to large proportions in these tangles of hawthorn and choke-cherry because hunters don't think of this as mule deer habitat.

Perhaps the second most neglected border is the one between high forests and alpine meadows. Granted, this border takes time and energy to reach. And if you get a deer here, it's a grunt and a half to pack it out. However, more big bucks per square mile live along this border than any other.

This is trophy country for good reason. Bucks are not bothered much on this border. They survive from year to year, and that, essentially, is much of what goes into growing large antlers. Because they aren't pushed around by hunting pressure, they don't have to expend much energy to fulfill their basic needs. Meadow grasses and forbs provide adequate nutrition, especially since there is little or no competition for food from does and fawns, which prefer borders at lower elevations. So bucks convert most of their groceries into growth.

This high border country is especially good to hunt early in the season before frosts and snow make finding food difficult for deer.

In between the low border of forest and farmland and the high border at timberline, there are a series of borders that occur mainly in response to elevation and its corresponding changes in climate. For example, as you climb a mountain in mule deer country you may go through aspen into spruce, then into lodgepole pine and Douglas fir, then into limber pine, whitebark pine, and finally into subalpine fir.

These are gradual borders with elevational bands in which vegetation communities intermingle, making them attractive to muleys.

The actual elevation at which you find specific species of trees dominating an area varies with latitude and aspect. For example, aspen trees are found at higher elevations in Colorado than in Idaho. And they grow higher on south-facing slopes, with their greater exposure to sunlight, than on north-facing slopes. But wherever they are found, these borders produce the variety and density of food and cover that muleys seek out.

Of all the borders, these are the least distinct. You need to be in tune with the trees around you while you hunt. Look for places where there are a variety of different species. When you get into an area where there is a monotony of lodgepole pine or fir, for example, you've left the border zone behind.

My favorite kind of border, however, is the type that occurs within a single-species stand. Mule deer hunting can be at its best, especially for bucks, where soil and moisture changes allow small islands of different vegetation to grow within a larger expanse of single-species forest.

For instance, moist draws extending up into otherwise dry country may allow fingers of aspen to poke back into great blocks of fir or lodgepole forest. The borders formed by these draws are often relatively small in size and may not supply enough forage for a large group of does and fawns. But a few bucks can prosper quite nicely by crossing back and forth between conifer and deciduous trees to bed and feed.

Lodgepole pine fills up most of the country where I usually hunt mule deer. But within these big stretches of forest, I've scouted out a series of moist bottoms and rocky ridges where secluded meadows, brushy hillsides, and grassy islands exist. In linking my hunting rounds to these diverse pockets of vegetation, I've found that I see a predominance of bucks.

In one remote pothole meadow, I caught sight of the same 4x5 buck a half-dozen times in one season before I finally outfoxed him. He lived on a border that couldn't have been more than an eighth of a mile in circumference.

So far, all the borders I've mentioned have been natural borders, but there are thousands of miles of manmade borders produced by logging. Their attraction to mule deer is not universal. New clearcuts often do not have a large enough variety of well-developed forage plants growing at their borders to attract deer in numbers. Old cuts may be too overgrown. Also, logging roads that remain open often carry enough traffic to scare off muleys. However, where cuts are small and roads are closed and where the bordering timber is thick, muleys may find an excellent border-crossing situation for a number of years, starting several years after the area is logged.

Clearly, borders can be found from the low foothills up to timberline, and knowing which hunting tactics to use along each type is largely a matter of knowing how and when different borders are used by muleys.

Those abrupt borders found between cropland and forest are crossed primarily at dawn and dusk, giving deer the security of low light when they're on the open side of the border. These are places mule deer can be effectively hunted from a stand if there are obvious points where they cross the border.

Not long ago I was hunting elk on a high knoll of winter range overlooking half a mile of alfalfa field. With a light covering of snow on the field, I could see tracks radiating out from a single spot where the field bordered a mixture of hawthorn and fir. It looked like a typical whitetail situation, but standing

In arid country, a transitional zone between plant communities may be as simple as a gentle draw, but the deer always know where to find these spots—and so should you. (Rodney Schlecht)

near that border crossing one evening a week later, I discovered muleys by the dozen.

Still-hunting, of course, is the more conventional means of going after muleys. And it can be used along borders at any time of day. You'll want to move parallel to the border, however, not back and forth across it. Where an abrupt border occurs between open country and wooded country, still-hunt along the wooded side. Otherwise, hunt as close to the center of the border as possible.

Gradual borders, where you may have a band of mixed vegetation an eighth to a quarter of a mile wide, can be still-hunted in a zigzag fashion. But realize that typical feeding times will find deer more in the heart of mixed vegetation, and bedding times will put them in the thicker single-species edges.

Up along timberline borders you'll want to sit and scout from a vantage point that overlooks a large area of alpine meadows. Muleys are prone to move about more during the day on these remote borders. So you can glass them while they feed and pinpoint where they cross into cover to bed.

Don't overlook the small island borders formed by clumps of stunted conifer in the midst of open meadows. They may look too small to deserve attention, but muley bucks love to bed in these niches.

Through binoculars, I once watched two bucks feeding on grass a quarter of a mile away on the side of a gradual alpine bowl. Around midmorning, one of them nosed into a clump of gnarled subalpine fir no bigger than my own bedroom. Minutes later the other buck entered a similar island of nearby fir.

Forty-five minutes after that, coming down on these borders from above, I jumped both bucks from their beds and had to make a quick choice between the two as they raced for the border of timberline 100 yards away.

Borders. They offer muleys a variety of foods and a diversity of cover. They offer muley hunters an excellent center of focus for the hunt.

THOSE ARE THE BREAKS

Lou Petroff is a tall man with a long handsome face topped by a shock of white hair. He talks with a quiet, decisive tone that suggests an even temperament and a thoughtful disposition. There is even a hint about him of someone comfortably set in his ways. Some of those ways are worthy of attention, if you happen to be looking for mule deer in the breaks country of the Great Plains.

Lou first appeared on my horizon while I was muttering imprecations over a flat tire in the middle of a sagebrush expanse at the edge of the Missouri River breaks in north-central Montana. He came out of a shallow swale with his rifle slung from his shoulder just as I was discovering that my spare was also flat. My heat was tempered by his cool.

"My son Gary can take you into town later. Why don't you just leave the whole headache here for now? I'm Lou Petroff. Come on down to camp. You might want to bring your rifle."

When good fortune follows bad, you don't ask many questions. I introduced myself and followed Lou down the gentle sagebrush slope toward a clump of juniper. ·

There was, however, one question I had to ask. It was a question Petroff did not find surprising, just a bit amusing from the perspective of a man who'd spent almost three decades hunting the breaks for mule deer from Montana to Texas.

"Were you really hunting in that little swale back there?"

Lou's smile was mercifully uncondescending. "I was."

"You were hunting for muleys, were you? Way out there in the sagebrush?"

"Well," Lou admitted, "I was only hunting *one* kind of muley."

I looked at him.

"Great big bucks," he grinned.

I couldn't help shaking my head in disbelief.

"Have you ever hunted around here before?" I shook my head no. "Have you ever hunted any breaks before?" I shook my head again. "Well, the breaks are like no other place you're likely to hunt. I've been at it for twenty-seven years. They take some getting used to."

Wherever the Great Plains first start to fall away to the larger rivers of the West and Midwest, erosion has made a labyrinth of the land. Starting sometimes six to eight miles from river bottoms, shallow coulees begin to finger through sagebrush flats similar to the one where Lou Petroff came upon me. As these drainage heads descend toward rivers, they deepen. And by the time they have reached the flood plains, the elevations between ridgetops and coulee bottoms may have reached hundreds of feet.

Extensive breaks country is found along the Missouri River in Montana, the Little Missouri River in North Dakota, and the Cheyenne and White Rivers in South Dakota. But lesser breaks can be found wherever rivers etch the Great Plains as they cut their swath through the midsection of the country from Canada to the Texas panhandle.

Of course, the Plains themselves are mostly rolling grassland, not typical mule deer country at all. That's why the bulk of the muley population of the Plains take up residence along the edges where the breaks offer the more rugged terrain that these hearty deer tend to favor.

Lou lit a burner on his propane stove and put on a pot of coffee. The camp was neat and comfortable, with a large green canvas tent and a rainfly pitched over the kitchen.

"I knew you were a newcomer when you asked me about hunting that draw back there. Every year, Gary and I watch most of the hunters head for the heart of the breaks. They want to get into the timber. It seems like the natural thing to do. We did the same thing for a number of years."

By now, of course, Lou really had an attentive audience, and he knew it.

Generally, the use of the breaks by mule deer seems to be motivated by their preference for good escape cover. The greater the relief of the topography, the safer they feel. That's the theory, anyway.

In the Missouri River breaks, and in most breaks like them, the wetter north-facing slopes support the thickest growth of Douglas fir and Rocky Mountain juniper, with an understory of Western snowberry along with chokecherry, silver sagebrush, and green rabbitbrush. These areas are ideal for bedding and escape cover, in addition to cover from the wind

Cagey mule deer bucks will use the thick cover of north-facing slopes as escape cover in the breaks. (Rodney Schlecht)

and heat. The north slopes also provide the most succulent food as the summer progresses and the more southern slopes dry out.

South-facing slopes are naturally drier, with sparser patches of fir and juniper and an understory dominated by skunkbush. These slopes hold less snow in the winter, giving the deer a good place to move about and to warm themselves.

In the heart of the breaks, a deer might only have to travel a few hundred feet to cross from one slope to another. So all the comforts and necessities of life are within easy reach.

"Ten years ago, I could take you into the steepest part of any breaks and show you all kinds of deer," Petroff said without bragging. "Any day of the season, I could go into those places and shoot a nice young buck. We could do it this afternoon."

He sipped the last of his coffee in silence and rinsed out both of our cups. "Let's go hunting. Gary won't be back for a couple of hours."

We did not head for the heart of the breaks. We cut out across the sagebrush to the start of a gentle coulee. Lou put me in the lead as we started down the easy slope. I did what I was told and kept my eyes open.

The sides of the coulee gradually rose as we descended. Clumps of snowberry and wild rose started to appear. The draw offered more protection than I'd expected. It seemed intimate and cloistered in surroundings that looked so exposed from the road.

The juniper was thicker now along both rims of the coulee, and Lou suggested we move up to walk those edges, one on each side. Perhaps he had wanted to see how I handled myself with a rifle before he let me walk anywhere except in front of him, but his only comment was to watch for the small openings among the juniper where deer might be feeding.

After an hour of careful, slow walking we'd seen nothing that resembled a mule deer. Lou was not apologetic. "It all takes time." That was his only comment as we headed back to camp. He knew I was about to burst at the seams, and he seemed to enjoy it.

"Okay," I finally gave in. "What's the story?"

My question was answered, in part, by a big four-point muley that Lou's son had just brought into camp in the back of a pickup. Lou introduced Gary.

"First-Time Coulee?" he questioned.

Gary nodded. "Right below Rocky Bend."

I had purchased the most detailed maps I could find of the area, and only a few of the larger drainages were named. The two men could have been talking about another country for all I could figure out. But Lou knew he'd about played things to an end, and he relented.

After they'd been hunting the heart of the breaks for half a dozen years, they'd begun to worry. They'd gotten their deer every year, but big bucks seemed to be in very short supply. Then one day on a hunch Lou had followed a deep coulee from the middle of the breaks all the way to where it almost disappeared below an access road that cut across an open sagebrush flat. There he jumped the biggest mule deer buck he'd seen in years, not fifty yards from the road.

Lou's hunch had been based on a sense of the mule deer's home range. He'd figured bucks would have a larger range than does and that they might tend to wander farther from the heartland of the breaks.

In fact, I have learned since meeting Lou that the difference between doe and buck ranges is considerable in this area. While does tend to stick to a modest range of between $1\frac{1}{2}$ and $2\frac{1}{2}$ square miles, mature bucks often use from 10 to 12 square miles.

It seems that some of this wide-ranging tendency is dependent on the weather. In the summer, when the temperatures really stoke up on the Great Plains, the flatter, more exposed areas take the brunt of the heat. Deer seek relief in the more rugged sections of the breaks where trees and terrain provide shade.

In the winter, those more exposed areas are equally inhospitable. With nothing to stop it, the wind whips across these places, sending wind-chill factors into the basement and piling so much snow in the shallow heads of coulees that they disappear.

Weather in the autumn, however, offers more far-ranging opportunities. The scorching temperatures of the summer have moderated, making the gentler, less-vegetated fringes of the breaks quite tolerable, especially during early and late daylight hours.

With all this in mind, and with their first big "breaks" buck on the wall, Lou and Gary Petroff decided to concentrate their hunting on these seldom worked outer edges.

"I guess we've been pretty methodical about it," Lou admits. "Whether we're hunting here or in the Dakotas or in Nebraska, we stick to three or four coulees. That way we get to know them fairly well."

You'll occasionally jump a nice buck like this one when you work slowly down through coulees and draws. (Rodney Schlecht)

His understatement is clear only after you've hunted with the Petroffs for a while. They seem to know every deer crossing, every juniper opening, every thicket, every bend, wrinkle, and outcropping of every coulee they hunt.

Their intimate knowledge of their hunting grounds has allowed the Petroffs to do "better than the average hunter," Gary says with the modesty of his father. But he also admits that *knowing* the big bucks are there and hunting with patience are probably the biggest secrets to their success.

"I don't know how many hunters we've watched drive by our camps over the past twenty years, but probably a quarter of them also drove within 100 yards of some big old buck lying down among the sage or juniper out there." Gary says, shaking his head. "Some guys even see some of those bucks once in a while, but most of them don't believe bucks oughta be in this open country, so they don't bother to hunt it."

Although the Petroffs' hunting tactics are mainly a matter of persistence, they usually like to hunt as a team. Sometimes, they'll walk down along the rims of a coulee, one on each side, the way Lou and I had done. They can look down into the coulee bottom, and then can scan the surrounding tableland for bucks feeding in openings among the juniper and sage. It's the most efficient way to cover the most country.

At other times, one of them will take a position at the head of a coulee while the other walks down away from the drainage edge for roughly a quarter of a mile and then works back up the coulee bottom. Then they'll walk down to where the first driver began, and he'll take a position there while the other man goes down another quarter of a mile and works back.

They never descend a coulee into the heart of the breaks unless they happen to be hunting during the rut. Then their tactics are different. Because the bucks are looking for does at this time of year (in the Missouri River breaks from around November 15 to December 10, with a peak between November 25 and 30), they spend more time in the steeper sections of the breaks where the does hang out. And they are constantly on the move.

The Petroffs have found the most effective way to hunt these bucks in rut is to get on a high point of ground and glass down into the rougher areas closer to the river bottoms. Dawn and dusk are the best times, and their sit-and-wait strategy is based on the fact that many a big buck will service does in the heartland all day and then come back to the fringes of the breaks to cool their heels at night.

"Hunting those rutty bucks is okay, if you don't mind spending most of your time sitting on your duff with a pair of binoculars. But I'd rather be walking," Lou confesses. "That's why I like to hunt the breaks early in the season. You can walk out these shallower draws where the terrain isn't too tough on your legs. And if you keep at it, just slowly working a few coulees you've gotten to know, you'll come up with a pretty good buck; sometimes a real good one."

I thought about Lou's advice that evening when Gary drove me in to get my tires fixed. On the way back, Gary said I'd better spend the night at their camp. It was too dark to get to where I might be going, he said.

Three days later, I was still spending the nights at the Petroffs' camp, thanks to their continued kind invitation. During the day, Gary introduced me to more of the intricacies of their coulees, claiming he had filled his tag and had nothing else to do. Lou spent the time hunting on his own.

Early on the fourth morning, I found a hefty three-point in a patch of wild rose near a game crossing Gary led me to. Thanks to my four days with the Petroffs, my success did not come as a surprise.

Back at camp, Lou laughed. "I won't even say I told you so."

He had seen another three-point in First-Time Coulee—a name derived from the fact that it was the first place he'd discovered a big buck on the outer edges of the breaks. He had passed up the three-point in favor of a chance to find a bigger buck he knew was there. Somewhere. It was just a matter of time. Lou already had the patience, and so should you if you hunt the breaks for trophy mule deer.

Hunting rutting bucks such as this often means getting on a high point and glassing riverbottoms and coulees, looking for bucks chasing does. (Bill McRae)

DEER ON THE GRASSLANDS

The Great Plains make up the largest habitat in the country for hunting mule deer. The mixed and short-grass prairies roll over portions of Montana, North and South Dakota, Colorado, New Mexico, Texas, Nebraska, Kansas, and Oklahoma, and they spill into parts of the Canadian provinces of Alberta, Saskatchewan, and Manitoba. The prairie represents the largest patch of grassland in North America. It's the land where, as the song goes, "the deer and the antelope play, where seldom is heard a discouraging word, and the skies are not cloudy all day."

Like many aspects of the West, however, there tends to be more myth than reality to the song.

Mule deer certainly do play, but they don't frolic out on the rolling grasslands that make up the vast majority of what we call the prairies. As a matter of fact, they don't like the grasslands much at all. Mule deer, when reality is given a say, probably occupy something like one-fifth of the landscape of the Great Plains, and it's a very specific one-fifth.

As for the bit about discouraging words, you should have heard the things that came out of my mouth the first time I tried hunting muleys on the prairie. But that's a story I won't go into. It's enough to say the cloudless skies dropped so much moisture that the prairie siltstone soil turned into what the folks in eastern Montana call "gumbo." In consistency it is not unlike a thick Creole soup, although the taste cannot compare. Gumbo is not easy to walk in or to drive in. It can send you home deerless, even if you've been looking for them in the right places.

When the truth comes out, there are lots of surprises on the prairies, especially when it comes to hunting mule deer.

The second time I went hunting on the prairie, I went with Charlie Breckenridge. Charlie teaches Social Studies in eastern Montana during the week. On weekends he hunts. He's had more time—eleven years of weekends—to figure out prairie muleys than I have. And when, after my first mule deer foray to the Great Plains, I told him I didn't believe there were any muleys on the prairies, he said I was probably right. Talk about surprised.

"If I were a mule deer, I sure as thunder wouldn't stand out in the middle of all that grass waiting for lightning to strike. I'd find a tree to hide under."

I frowned at Charlie's irony.

"It's a fact, Sam, muleys want some cover. They aren't going to stand around on the open prairie waiting for you or me to come along on a brisk fall weekend. They want someplace to hide, and they want that place to come supplied with eats. There are not a heck of a lot of places on the prairies that can provide both cover and forage."

I sensed Charlie was starting a lecture, and I was his only student, but I didn't protest. So he told me about his first summer on the prairie.

Although hunting the grasslands can make you feel like you're searching for a needle in a haystack, early in the season you'll often find muley bucks hanging out around draws where tree and brush cover grows thick. (Rodney Schlecht)

It seems Charlie had expected to find mule deer playing around out in the grass, too. When he didn't find them there, he started poking around elsewhere. While driving the county roads in the evenings, he discovered dozens of muleys congregated in the alfalfa fields that are typically sandwiched between hardwood draws filled with green ash and chokecherry.

Now the alfalfa fields and the hardwood draws compose only a very small percentage of the available prairie landscape—maybe two or three percent each. But in combination they seemed, to Charlie, to provide everything necessary for a mule deer. Because the draws received and soaked up water from the surrounding terrain, they supported the only deciduous trees for miles around. The trees gave the muleys cover. Other vegetation in the draws, like snowberry and various grasses, provided forage. The adjacent alfalfa fields were a succulent dividend that could be reached without having to move far from the security of the trees.

"So that's where we should hunt them, right? Catch them in the open as they enter or leave the alfalfa fields?" I quizzed Charlie over dinner the night before our hunt.

"Oh, the muleys aren't in the alfalfa fields *now*." Charlie's tone let me know I had gotten ahead of myself. "By the time hunting season opens, the hay has all been harvested, and the stubble is as dry as a desert beer can. No, you don't want to use summer scouting to tell you where prairie muleys will be in the fall. As a matter of fact, right about now they are probably beginning to migrate."

Now Charlie has been known to pull a leg or two, and I had a feeling at least one of mine was being stretched. He must have sensed my disbelief.

"No kidding, Sam. They *are* migrating, at least a lot of them are. They migrate just like those muleys of yours over in the Bridger Mountains do. The only difference is that your muleys come downhill in the fall and ours go uphill."

I waited for the punchline that never came. Instead, I got a theory that seemed almost reasonable when I thought about it.

By the end of the summer, Charlie continued, not only the harvested hayfields but just about any vegetation that is exposed to the prairie sun gets pretty dried up. In search of the last succulent forage, the muleys keep to the hardwood draws on north slopes where the effects of the sun will be moderated. But there comes a time, usually somewhere between mid-

October and the end of November, when the muleys go on the move. They move to the badlands.

Prairie badlands are in the highlands. It's the hilly terrain that is steeper and more prone to erosion. And although it covers more territory than the hardwood draws—perhaps 15 percent of the entire prairie habitat—it is not what you'd call vast.

In any event, the mule deer head up to the badlands. They may gain only 300 or 400 feet in total elevation, but that often represents a move of four or five miles. Some muleys make the move overnight; others take a week to get there.

They are after the last vestiges of succulent forage, and though the badlands might seem a strange place to look for this, Charlie had an explanation.

The badlands are a jumble of eroded fingers facing in different directions, he pointed out. Three quarters of the twisted landscape is bare ground. Yet, as sparse as the vegetation is, it is more diverse than any other part of the prairie. And it stays green the longest because the steepness of the terrain and its variety moderate the summer sun's desiccating rays.

Like mule deer migrations in mountainous, prairie migration is prompted by weather. But instead of heavy snow and cold temperatures starting deer movement to the lowlands, it is drought and heat that move the prairie muleys up high to the badlands. The drier and hotter the summer has been, the earlier the deer will move up.

Once there, the mule deer stay until early spring, surviving on sagebrush, rabbitbrush, and juniper. Although heat and dryness push them into the badlands in the fall, it is the advent of real winter weather, especially snow, cold, and wind, which keeps them there. The rugged topography of the badlands stops most of the drifting snow around their periphery, leaving relatively calm, snow-free pockets within the interior. These are the spots where mule deer spend the winter.

"So where do we start hunting in the morning?" I asked when Charlie had finished his lesson.

"Well, it's been a hot summer out here," he answered, "but there are a couple of hardwood draws I've scoped out on a good northern slope. As of last weekend, there were still some bucks up there. I think it's worth a try. Besides the draws are a little easier to hunt than the badlands; they aren't quite as surprising."

Charlie wouldn't tell me what that meant. He said I'd have to find out for myself.

Before daybreak we had followed a gravel road in a straight line through the open prairie to a point where a rutted track turned up the backbone of a long low ridge.

"You don't want to drive this after a rain," Charlie said as the sky lightened. I offered him another cup of coffee from the thermos, but he had both hands on the steering wheel.

He parked the truck in a little dimple along the ridge, and we stepped out into the wind. Wind is a constant on the prairie; it averages ten to fifteen miles per hour all the time. It has been known to loosen the underpinnings of people's mental stability after they've been exposed to it day after day, weekend after weekend.

Charlie looked at the sky and commented to no one in particular that there was going to be a change in the weather.

When I asked him how he knew, he just shrugged and said he'd been living on the prairies long enough to feel it in the wind. For the first time, I thought I saw sort of a crazed look in Charlie's eyes, but that disappeared as soon as he started laying out his plan.

The north-slope hardwood draws are the last holdouts for the muleys before they migrate to the badlands, usually sometime during hunting season. If they were still there, they would probably be feeding on snowberry on the slopes of the draws. Like mule deer everywhere, they seem to prefer hillsides to bottomland. We would work opposite sides of the draw from the top to a point where trees obscured our view of one another. Then we'd regroup.

The plan sounded good, but there weren't any deer in the first draw or the second. By late morning we returned to the pickup for an early lunch. It felt good to get out of the wind. Charlie suggested we continue to work the north-slope draws for the rest of the day despite the apparent absence of deer.

"Muleys are pretty traditional in their use of an area. There may be deer in here that use only one or two branches of this whole north-slope drainage, and we may not have found those yet."

By the end of the day, however, we both agreed that the mule deer must have made their move to the badlands.

The next day the weather had changed. It was quite a bit colder, and I figured maybe Charlie wasn't nuts after all. But the wind was still there, blowing like a permanent part of the prairie environment.

As the season progresses, prairie mule deer migrate to the badlands where they can find shelter and food. (Rodney Schlecht)

Following the same gravel road as the day before, we passed the hardened gumbo track that went up the ridge and continued on for five or six miles, gradually gaining ground as the terrain began to break away on both sides of us.

When Charlie stopped the truck, it was just light enough to see the labyrinth of eroded coulees that spread out below us. Before he opened his door, Charlie gave me a short course on the wind.

"We aren't going to pay any attention to the windward slopes because the muleys won't have anything to do with them. On a day like today with the temperature in the low 40s, this wind will make it feel as if it's in the teens. So the deer are going to be bedding and feeding on the leeward side of these slopes. Even the sun on the south-facing slopes doesn't seem to entice them. I guess they just lose less heat by staying out of the wind."

Charlie had a few last instructions. "We'll work around the tops of these fingers so we can look down into the coulees. Keep a sharp eye out, and be ready for surprises." Something told me Charlie was having fun at my expense. But I did as I was told.

We followed the first finger out a quarter of a mile before it crumbled away to the coulee bottom. As we retraced our route, Charlie spoke against the wind. Even in the badlands the mule deer remain territorial, he said. They choose a combination of certain coulees for their winter range and ignore others that look just as good to you and me.

In the next coulee we routed out a doe and fawn. They pogo-sticked away through the sage and rabbitbrush. After three more return trips to the ends of fingers I was getting a bit weary, but Charlie wanted to try one more before going back to the truck. He urged me ahead of him, and I scanned the tan-colored earth that was interspersed with sparse clumps of vegetation.

The explosion took place about halfway out along the coulee. It was at a point where the sides of the coulee were almost perpendicular, and I couldn't really see the base of the drop. Suddenly, directly below *my* feet a four-point buck came snorting to *his* feet. He was so close I could see the muscles ripple on his shoulders as he made the first powerful lunge to get out from under me. His presence came as such a surprise that I lost several seconds getting a steady aim. But he was still close enough for a clean shot.

As the dust settled and I shook my head, Charlie's grin almost cracked his face. "I told you hunting up here could be surprising."

FINDING MULE
DEER WHEN
POPULATIONS
PLUMMET

Way back in the fall of 1983, I got a phone call from Turk Jaramus, a friend and hunting companion who had left Montana to take a job in northern Utah. Turk was all cranked up over the mule deer hunting down there. Muleys were coming out of the woodwork, he told me. I should drive down, he said, and he'd guarantee a fantastic weekend of hunting.

Unfortunately, a string of other commitments that fall put a stop to a trip south, but I promised Turk that I'd make time the following season to join him and all of those mule deer. The phone call I got the next fall, however, lacked the enthusiasm of the one from the previous year. Mule deer numbers had plunged from a peak in 1983 to a rock-bottom low in 1984. The experts were pointing to the unusually severe winter that year as the cause of the abrupt decline.

Despite the bad news and the fact that I could have found easier mule deer hunting in Montana, I told Turk that I'd come down anyway. There had to be some muleys left somewhere, we rationalized.

There were deer left in northern Utah that season, but not where they'd been in numbers the fall before. Driving along the open foothills, Turk nodded at the expansive landscape. "There were mule deer all over those hills last year at this time." We hadn't seen one in an hour of driving.

Both of us agreed that we'd have to get back into the trees before we found any of the deer that were left. And that's where we finally did connect with Utah's hard-time muleys.

Professional wildlife biologists are not entirely sure why mule deer populations go up and down. Predation, disease, habitat loss and conflicting land use certainly all play some part in the process. Perhaps most influential, however, are environmental conditions. Extremely cold winters with above-average snow depths can bring about a dramatic drop in deer numbers due to winter-kill. A string of hot, dry summers combined with tough winters can result in more gradual declines in populations due to poor fawn survival.

Hard times for mule deer populations occurred in the mid-1970s. The killer winter of 1983–84, which hit much of the West's mule deer range, had a devastating effect on many herds, which deer hunters certainly felt the following season. Mule deer numbers dropped hard again from 1995 to 1997.

For the mule deer hunter, population lows mean more than just fewer deer to hunt. It means that mule deer will no longer be found in some of the places where hunters found them before. In fact, they may survive only in specific niches of their range.

Even during hard times, however, there are mule deer to be hunted. The secret, according to wildlife biologist Dave Pac, is to find their core habitat.

"The way mule deer are distributed over their range starts with a core area," Pac said. "In many areas of the West, that is the mountain/foothill habitat. This is where a lot of does have set up their home range. They maintain themselves pretty well throughout time in this good-quality core habitat."

The fawns produced by these does have one main objective: to set up a home range right near Mom. And they do that until the core habitat is filled to capacity. Then fawns are forced to start setting up home ranges outside the core. They move down to the more open slopes near or on agricultural land or they go up to alpine country at or near timberline.

So at a peak in population, deer have filled the entire environment. They have filled it to peak density in the core habitat, and they have also filled up the marginal habitat to a fairly high degree.

"Now, let's say the environment changes," Pac hypothesized. "The winters get more severe, and the summers get drier. All of the deer are subjected to stress in achieving their resource needs. But the deer in the core area occupy a more diverse habitat, so they have more options. During a dry summer, they can pick and choose and find more wet sites where there's good for-

When mule deer populations drop off, you'll still find nice bucks if you seek out their core habitat. (Rodney Schlecht)

age. In the winter, they can find places that are free of snow and thus survive pretty well.

"But the deer on the margins have a tougher time. Snow piles up out on the edges, on the open foothills, and on the valley floors. It's hard to find good places to winter, and it gets awfully dry out there in the summer.

"After being under this stress for a couple of years, the deer on the margins begin to have very few fawns to reinforce their home range patterns. The population on the margins may drop right out of the picture.

"An individual deer doesn't have much flexibility. Once it's set up a home range that happens to be in marginal habitat, it is not going to take off and move up into the core habitat when things get tough. It is locked into its traditional patterns.

"A lot of people think that when times get tough, deer can pick up shop and move to where things are okay," Pac added. "That's not true. They're going to use all of their options on the home range they've established, and when they run out of these options, they're dead."

According to Pac, what a core habitat has that marginal areas don't is, first and foremost, a diversity of topographic features. It is country where hills and ridges and draws face in different directions. Each time there is a change in direction, there is a change in the plant communities. And each plant community has something that mule deer will be looking for sometime during the year.

Dave drew this analogy: "It's like the facets of a crystal. If you have a lot of facets, there is more sparkle. And deer in those core areas can pick up on all of that."

So, with a diversity of topography you get a diversity of vegetation. You also get places that will retain moisture even when it's dry. Northern slopes, deep ravines, and sequestered coulees will maintain lush green vegetation when more exposed places have already turned brown and crisp.

This stability is another key to core deer habitat. The longer an environment can sustain nutritious forage, the better it can support mule deer during hard times.

That's why the forested zone of the mountain-foothills area is so important. The forest is the place where forage remains green for the longest period of time. Although it greens up first on the low open foothills, it also dries out quickly there. Vegetation greens a little later under the forest canopy, but it is green into October. In the high country, on the other hand, it doesn't get green until mid-July, and it is often covered with snow by mid-September.

Though the forested mid-elevations of the mountain-foothills habitat provide the core areas of mule deer over much of the West, the prairies and breaks and deserts have their core areas as well. In areas east of the Rocky Mountains, fluctuations in weather patterns tend to vary more each year than they do west of the Continental Divide. Consequently, the ups and downs of a mule deer population are greater.

The key to core habitat in the prairie is the hardwood draws, where green ash, box elder, and hackberry form the typical overstory and where mule deer have the best chance of finding green forage—especially during the fall, when vegetation in most locations has turned brown and dry. Woody draws also provide protection from wind and drifting snow during severe fall storms.

These draws collect more moisture (through surface flow and subirrigation) than the amount that actually falls on the site, so they can provide nutritious forage longer than any other location on the prairie. Usually, the larger and deeper the draw, the better the core habitat it offers. If some or all of the draw faces north, that's another plus.

Where the prairies crumble away to the larger rivers, the relief of the topography increases. Erosion cuts creases in the Great Plains that start as shallow draws five or six miles back from the main drainage bottoms and grow to 800-foot-deep coulees just before they empty into the rivers. These are the badlands or the breaks of the West.

Research biologist Ken Hamlin, who studies mule deer distributions in the Missouri River breaks, said that the core habitat in this kind of country is back in the deep coulees close to the river. There, deer have access to the flood plain as well as the moist and shaded niches of the coulee bottoms.

Like the forested midsection of the mountain foothills and the woody draws of the prairies, the deep coulees provide the most diverse topography and, therefore, the most varied and long-lived vegetation. Like the other core habitats, the coulees also offer the greatest protection from the environmental extremes that are often initially responsible for declines in the mule deer populations.

In the desert, core areas cluster around any available water, where deer can find succulent forage, including deciduous shrubs. This usually means north slopes in broken high country.

Within these core areas, however, bucks usually do not occupy the same territory as do does and fawns, except during the rut. Perhaps it has been the long history of evolution that has conditioned mature bucks to avoid competing with does and fawns for forage and cover. The survival of the species is partially dependent on the avoidance of some competition, and the bucks seem to know this instinctively. "Bucks usually occupy the lower-quality habitat in a population," Dave Pac said. "Generally, this means that the bucks hang out on the habitat fringes."

In the mountain foothills, these areas are usually defined by elevation. Bucks stay in the lower foothills on forest edges near agricultural land, or they establish home range close to timberline. The harder the times, the closer toward the center

In the breaks, deer will retreat to deep coulees when times get tough.

of the core habitat the bucks will establish themselves. This sandwich social structure—bucks on the top and bottom, does in the center—has become the key for me when hunting muley bucks in mountain-foothill habitat.

In prairies and breaks, bucks are usually in the higher, shallower sections of the draws and coulees, while the does and fawns inhabit the moister, deeper areas that foster more vegetation and cover.

According to Pac, "We can't really generalize what it's going to look like from the prairies through the mountains. There are differences in what the lower-quality core habitat is going to look like, depending on the place. It's less timbered, however. Both the high and low elevations where bucks live in the mountain foothills are less timbered. It is less timbered where they live in the breaks, too. It's simpler habitat. That's the key."

It certainly was the key for Turk Jaramus and me when we hunted hard-time muleys in northern Utah during that 1984 season. Leaving the open foothills, tinted silver-green by the sage, we worked our way through an intricate network of graveled county roads into a mixed woodland of juniper and piñon. Higher up, mountain mahogany, Gambel oak, pine, and fir made up the center of the core habitat in this area. We decided, however, to work the less wooded draws at lower elevations.

It was not easy hunting. All day we worked parallel draws from top to bottom until we ran out of juniper. Then we'd work up another set of draws until we started getting into oak and pine. It was a methodical process; we figured that in times of low deer populations, it was the best way to comb the area for whatever bucks that might be left there.

Late on the first afternoon, our tactics paid off. Ahead of me, a four-pointer came over the ridge at a trot, perhaps pushed by Turk's movement in the next draw. It was the first deer I'd seen all day.

Hearing my shot, Turk arrived twenty minutes later. "Not the easiest hunting ever, but at least we didn't get skunked," he said with a grin. The next day, we *did* get skunked using the same tactics. And the day after that, I had to head home.

The following Monday, I got a phone call from Turk. He'd decided to try a different tactic and had packed a light camp into the high country for the weekend. Up among the clumps of subalpine fir, he'd glassed the terrain at dawn and dusk and during the midday poked around the edges of islands of fir, hoping to spook a bedded buck.

Just before he was going to hike out to his truck on Sunday afternoon, a buck stepped out from behind some firs, and Turk ended his mule deer season. Although his success came high and mine low, what we both remember about that season is that we had to hunt hard on the fringes of core habitat to find those hard-time muleys. It's a lesson I always remember when mule deer populations plummet.

Habits That Give Mule Deer Away

DINING WITH
MULE DEER

" Find a good place it can eat, and you'll find a good muley."
That bit of advice comes back to me as clearly as the
day it was spoken, despite the passage of decades. The stubble-
chinned old man who told me that has passed on to other
places, but you can bet I believed what he said that cold autumn day as I stood beside his weathered barn, which bristled
with assorted mule deer racks.

His advice sounds simplistic, but after you've worked it
over for years, you realize it goes to the heart of good hunting
sense. Eating takes up more time than any other activity in a
mule deer's day. Chances are, the last muley you took was in
the middle of a meal. So it only stands to reason that where
mule deer eat is a key factor in hunting success.

During the fall, when hunting season opens, mule deer are
pretty picky about where they chow down. Generally, the good
places to eat at this time of year are going to be under the cover
of trees and/or on the north slopes of hillsides, draws, or coulees.

Think about it.

Despite the widespread belief that mule deer live on twigs
and branches, they'll go for succulent forbs over browse any

day. And if they have to eat deciduous browse, they'd much prefer it with leaves on rather than reduced to bare twigs.

Given this menu preference, muleys have a limited number of places they can eat.

Consider the foothills and mountains that make up much of their range. By fall, heat and frost have done in most of the succulent forage that is out in the open on the low foothills or the high alpine meadows. But under the sparse timber at mid-elevations where plants have taken longer to sprout in the spring, preferred forbs like dandelions, asters, goldenrod, and arnica are still green and succulent in October.

For a while, on timbered south and west slopes, muleys can find their favorite food under cover where frost hasn't yet reached. But as cold weather increases, the deer shift more and more to north-slope timber, where a thicker understory of such shrubs as snowberry and huckleberry still hold some of their leaves.

This north-slope timber, providing it has healthy understory browse, is where I hunt mule deer in the foothills. It's a congregating place for muleys looking for the most nutritious food left before winter really sets in. The more snow you find accumulated on these northern slopes, the farther down on them the deer will move.

So a survey of your local hunting grounds for good muley eating places should take into consideration the influence of weather on both food palatability and deer movement.

When the old man by the barn gave me his advice, he never told me to hunt north-slope timber. So I spent a number

Mountain mule deer have a hard time foraging in deep snow. (Rodney Schlecht)

of years wandering around other parts of the forest where I'd seen deer eating at other times of year. But fall is a definite transition in feeding routines, and the observations I'd made during other seasons didn't suggest that muleys would have special feeding niches during the time I could go out and hunt them.

Nevertheless, north-slope feeding in the fall seems to hold true no matter what the habitat. That vast intermountain area filled with sagebrush is no exception. While most of this area has turned crisp after months of summer heat, the north slopes of juniper and piñon draws at higher elevations still hold succulent forage. The bigger and deeper the draw, the more muleys it seems to hold.

When you move out on the real plains, you'll still find muleys seeking out north slopes, but sometimes that means going to higher elevations and sometimes it means going down low. Where the Great Plains break up into eroded fingers that fall away to big rivers, mule deer move down low into these bottom badlands in the fall. Their steep-sided, north-slope ravines maintain green vegetation long after more exposed tableland has turned brown and crisp.

Away from the rivers, however, a mule deer's first move in the fall will be into north-slope hardwood where deer have the best chance of finding green forage. These natural drainage areas hold more water than actually falls on them because of runoff and subsurface irrigation, so they contain succulent, tasty forage longer than most other locations.

But when cold, snowy weather sets in on the prairie before the end of the hunting season, mules are going to move up high. These higher, steeper areas are more prone to the erosion that characterizes local badlands with the deep gullies and diverse aspects. Here, on north slopes, sparse but varied vegetation offers the best eating a muley can find under harsh conditions.

Although north slopes are the rule for eating hotspots during hunting season, there are some exceptions, and there are some additional places you should check out.

In very heavily forested areas where dense tree canopies block out most of the sunlight, little understory vegetation grows no matter what the direction of the slope. The only time I've found this kind of forest cover offering good hunting is in stands of Douglas fir after a storm has broken off that year's new branch growth and blown them to the ground. At these times, I've seen mule deer move into thick forests in numbers to eat branch tips off the snow.

Otherwise, the deer depend on the edges of small openings to provide good eating opportunities in thick forests. In the mature and old-growth timber that produce dense forest canopies, openings caused by windthrow, insect damage, or just old age are often numerous.

The thick lodgepole forest near my home was hit a decade ago by an infestation of the pine bark beetle. Pockets of mature trees, whose trunks were girdled by the beetle, eventually died, making windows of sunlight in an otherwise dark and unproductive forest. These areas now attract mule deer in the fall because of the deciduous shrubs that have begun to grow there.

More recently, an unusually wet, heavy May snowstorm snapped the tops off numerous lodgepoles and uprooted many old fir trees. Where this natural thinning process has taken place, mule deer have begun to find new growth of fall food, and I've begun to find new niches to hunt muleys.

Perhaps the biggest stimulant to food growth is fire, whether it occurs in mountain forests, sagebrush hills, or rolling

After fire sweeps through an area, the grass that grows back provides excellent nutrition for mule deer and other species.

prairie. It has long been known that fire destroys old, unproductive vegetation and adds nutrients to the soil, which in turn foster the growth of new vigorous browse species. But what attracts mule deer long before any shrubs get big enough to eat is grass growth in the fall after a fire. First, fire clears away thick mats of old, dead ground litter that choke out grass at any time of year. Second, it blackens the soil, allowing it to warm more due to the increased absorption of sunlight. This warming nurtures the growth of cool season grasses—grasses like Kentucky bluegrass, cheatgrass, and bluebunch wheatgrass—throughout the fall and even into winter.

Where fire causes this fall grass growth, the area becomes the Ritz for mule deer in search of the last vestiges of succulent food. The protein content of this green grass may be more than twenty-five percent while most of the other available forage at this time of year averages three to five percent.

So be on the lookout for natural or manmade burns wherever you hunt mule deer. It doesn't have to be a big burn. Last summer, one of my ranching neighbors spent a wet day in September cleaning out a section of irrigation ditch that runs near his home. As part of that process, he torched the overgrown grassy banks, which managed to burn despite the dampness. By the time deer season opened, lush green grass six inches high carpeted the sides of the ditch, and mule deer came there to eat as if it were a feeding trough. Because of that burn, I could be fussy last year about waiting for just the right antlers to come along.

Bowhunter with velvet-antlered buck he took near burned-over area in Utah. (Lee Kline)

Let me mention one last eating hangout that may surprise you—the powerline right-of-way. No kidding. Those giant towers that carry wires from sea to shining sea through the thick of vast forests also shelter some of the best mule deer forage around. While the forest through which it runs may be dense and unproductive, the power line right-of-way must be kept cut down to early stages of vegetative growth. That means lots of young, tender shrubs.

In addition, because the right-of-way is long and narrow, there is a disproportionate percentage of "edge," that zone where one type of habitat abuts another. Along this edge, just inside the timber, plants get enough sunlight to grow well, but they are also protected from early frosts. It's a good place for muleys to eat, so it's a good place to hunt muleys, to paraphrase an old man with a barnside full of big racks.

BEDDING-SITE BUCKS

During the fall, mule deer go on a major eating binge to stock up on fat reserves for winter. They know that if they don't put on some extra pounds when forage is still relatively easy to find, they may not have enough body fat to carry them through the late winter and early spring, a time when food is difficult to find at best.

For muleys, the eating process is a two-step affair that centers around their bedding sites. They move around to gather edibles, then retire to their beds to digest their food and chew their cuds, or ruminate. By examining the dynamics of a mule deer's gathering and digesting routines, you can get some good leads on specific places to hunt them.

In order to convert food into fat efficiently in the fall, muleys tend to limit their movements to a small area where they are familiar with the available forage and bedding sites that they can use during various kinds of weather.

For example, a mule deer near a good food supply during favorable weather conditions may spend any given twenty-four-hour period within an area of only 200 to 300 square yards. Last year I saw the same hook-antlered buck in the same draw at seven o'clock in the morning and four o'clock in the afternoon. The draw was loaded with snowberries, and the day was cool and windless. The buck could forage and ruminate without expending much energy, thereby getting the most out of his food intake.

In many habitats the daily area a mule deer needs to cover to consume sufficient food may be more like 500 to 600 square yards, or roughly a third of a mile. Nevertheless, that distance is still a very manageable area in which to hunt deer.

During the course of a day, a deer typically feeds near a bedding site before it lies down to ruminate, and it also feeds near the site when it gets up. This leads to a definite block of time when its activities are concentrated around a specific base of operation—its bed.

For example, studies suggest that the average bedding time for a mule deer is around forty-five minutes and that deer may feed near the bedding site for approximately the same length of time before and after ruminating. This translates to roughly two hours when a mule deer may be in a very limited area centered around a bed.

Within the course of a day a mule deer may spend several hours around three or four bedding sites, usually eating its way from one to another. Each of these bases of operation may cover only 150 to 200 square yards.

In addition, on any given mule deer home range the number of bedding sites that are suitable for specific weather conditions are limited. These sites are likely to be used over and over again. In most cases, repeated use of these sites does not deplete the food supply because muleys are haphazard eaters. They take a few bites of this bush and a few bites of that grass, and then they move on to something else. So the same area can be used many times without exhausting the entire food stock. As a result, if you know where the bedding sites are, you have an excellent start on pinpointing mule deer whereabouts.

The time of day when deer are likely to use specific sites is largely dependent on the weather. For example, in the mountain-foothill habitat typical of a large portion of the mule deer's range, certain topographical features and vegetation offer protection from various weather conditions at different times of day. What follows is a look at likely mule deer movements at various temperatures.

Cool nights/warm days. At the beginning of the season when the weather is often moderate, muleys may spend the early hours of the morning feeding and bedding out in the open. As the temperature warms, they'll seek some shade, but they tend to favor sparse forest overstories where they can still find food. When it cools again in late afternoon, the deer leave the shade and head for openings where food is abundant, perhaps bedding down near a lone tree or a clump of low bushes.

Frosty nights/mild days. With the coming of frosty nights, the deer usually shift their evening and morning bedding sites to high ground to avoid pockets of cold air that collect in valley and canyon bottoms. During this type of weather muleys may surprise you by occupying their favorite lowland feeding grounds in the middle of the day because the temperature is more comfortable there at that time.

One fall I bumbled into three bucks bedded in a low-lying glade at the edge of a hayfield. It was late in the morning, and I was hurrying to get to the top of the draw where I'd spotted a

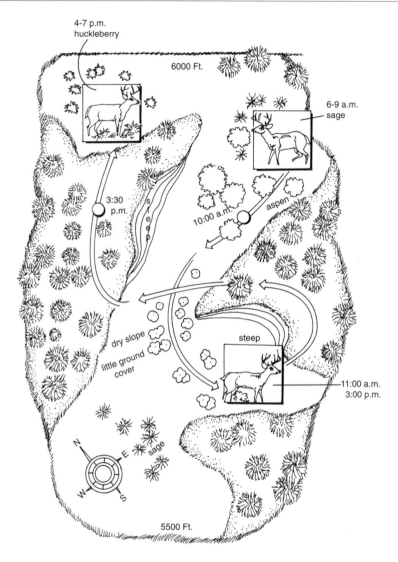

During frosty nights and mild days, mule deer select morning and evening bedding sites at high elevations to avoid pockets of cold air that form in valley and canyon bottoms. Midday they may surprise the hunter by bedding down in their favorite lowland feeding grounds where the temperature is to their liking.

lone buck the night before. Frankly, I wasn't thinking about the influence of weather on bedding sites, and this ruined my chance at the pick of three nice bucks.

Windy, cold nights and days. Nothing does more to concentrate mule deer at certain bedding sites than the combination of wind and cold temperatures. The home range of most muleys will have a limited number of places where protection from both wind and cold is provided and where forage is also available. Deer seek steep leeward slopes to block the wind, and they try to combine a windbreak with some forest overstory to decrease radiant heat loss. During the middle of the day they may move out in the open if the sun is shining and they can maintain protection from the wind.

Frigid nights/cold days. It's during extreme cold that muleys will head for thick timber. Even though little or no food is available in these heavily canopied areas, deer can minimize energy loss by staying under cover at night and in the early morning and late afternoon. In this frigid weather, I have come upon groups of deer clustered in the thickest part of the forest, often bedded up against the trunks of the largest trees where the temperature may have been a few degrees warmer than the surrounding air. At these times the deer are reluctant to move, and they stay bedded well into the day.

Along with knowing the general types of locations a mule deer is likely to use for bedding in varying weather, scouting out specific bedding sites and deciding when they might be used will increase your ability to locate deer.

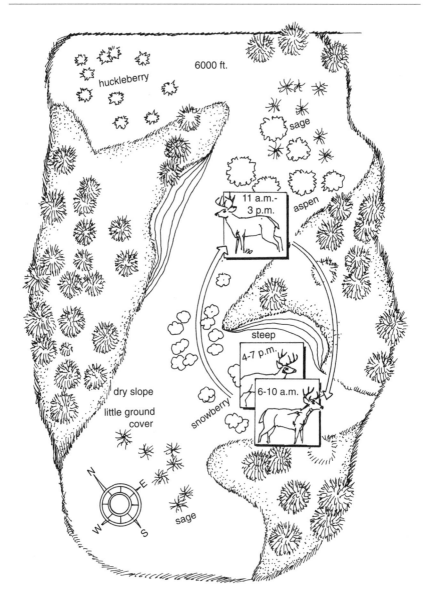

When cold, windy days and nights prevail, muley bedding sites are limited to those few spots offering both protection and forage. Often, these havens are located on steep, leeward slopes with a forest overstory to reduce radiant heat loss. If the sun is shining and they can avoid the wind, the deer may move out into the open.

Beds on sloping terrain—a favorite spot for muleys—are often easy to find because mule deer paw earth and ground litter to the downhill side in order to create a level area. I once discovered nine such beds within 100 feet of one another just below the leeward crest of a ridge. I returned to the spot one windy morning to find two bucks chewing their breakfast.

The times when muleys will be using their bedding sites are not as arbitrary as you might think. One mule deer study put the daily peaks of rest between 7 and 8 A.M., 10 and 11 A.M., 1 and 2 P.M., and 3 and 4 P.M. Even with seasonal shifts in these peaks, there were still definite bedding periods in the early and late morning and in the early and late afternoon. Moreover, the absence or presence of moonlight seems to have no influence on the time mule deer feed or bed.

The existence of peak bedding periods suggests another characteristic of mule deer behavior that works in favor of the hunter. Individual deer are influenced by the activities of other deer in the area, so there is a kind of group cohesion. If several deer bed down to ruminate, the rest of the deer in the group usually join them. Likewise, once a few deer have risen from their beds and have started foraging, it is very unlikely that any of the others are going to stay in bed and be left behind. As a result, you find groups of deer, not just individuals, bedding and eating at about the same times—a phenomenon that makes the prospect of hunting bedding sites for mule deer all the more attractive.

TRAILS THAT LEAD TO MULE DEER

The game trails that lace the Western forests are ideal pathways for both mule deer and mule deer hunters. Although muleys do not use game trails with nearly the regularity that whitetails do, the trails are indicators of well-used habitat. Equally important is the fact that game trails are often the only quiet places to walk when the rest of the woods are covered with dried leaves and litter.

Using game trails to pursue mule deer makes sense in four specific places.

HILLSIDES

Muleys love hillsides. They are obstacles in the path of would-be pursuers. While the mule deer goes up the hill with graceful bounds, man and other beasts pant and stumble far behind. So muleys hang out on hillsides. And when they aren't being pursued, they move up and down hills in the way that demands the least exertion of lungs and muscles—they traverse. They move across the face of a hillside at a gradual up or down angle. It's not the shortest route from top to bottom, but it sure gets them there with the least expenditure of energy.

The hillside trails that deer leave behind after repeated used are a boon to hunters. You can walk up and down them

On steep hillsides, deer will usually create trails that traverse the terrain at a gentle grade. (Rodney Schlecht)

quietly. They allow you to cover the entire face of a hillside in search of your game. They afford a relatively flat, cleared place to walk so you aren't dislodging stumps and rocks that go thumping down the hill. And when snow is on the ground, these trails may be the only way to hunt hillsides while standing erect.

The few foolish times I've tried hunting steep hillsides in snow without staying on game trails I have (1) turned an ankle, (2) turned into a snowman, and (3) turned back.

If you are lucky, you just "come on" these hillside trails; more often you have to scout for them. The best way to do this is to march (struggle) straight up or down the fall line. When you find a trail, follow it, and file its location in your head. I've memorized a whole series of hillside trails on my favorite mule deer grounds, and I inevitably use several of them whenever I hunt.

There is one notable quirk to these hillside pathways: Sometimes a perfectly clear train will peter out only to start up again ten or twenty yards up or down the hill. This break is usually caused by an obstruction of some sort that deer detour around, taking any number of random routes so that no clear trail is formed. Most of the time you can pick up a clear trail again by sighting a line on where the trail would have gone if it had continued unobstructed.

THICK BRUSH AND TIMBER

While hillsides are great places to hunt muleys, thick brush and timber are not. Visibility is limited, movement is difficult, and progress can be cursingly slow. Still, game trails often cut into these jungles, and they can open a way for you to scramble through tangles you might otherwise have to detour around or claw noisily through.

Wherever I hunt, I'm always looking for trails in the bottom of ravines where moisture makes for thick vegetation that may not be too wide but that may run the entire length of the draw. A well-placed game trail in such a situation can save a half-hour detour.

Don't plan to hunt on these trails, though. You may have to do some hunkering and even some crawling to get through these places that deer take in stride. (Deer always have a way of reminding us of our shortcomings, our clumsiness, our dulled senses.) Trails through the thick of things are not hunting trails; they are shortcuts to happier hunting grounds. So keep your rifle's chamber empty. Encircling brush has a way of playing with your safety and your trigger. And the deadfalls you may have to mount and dismount while pursuing game trails through thick timber can dump you on your duff as surely as a stubborn horse.

I didn't say all game trails would be easy. They may just be less difficult than other alternatives.

SADDLES AND PASSES

Saddles and passes are great places to find well-worn game trails. They are natural byways between drainages, and they funnel deer traffic through a very restricted area. You are likely to find one main game trail in these spots that looks like something Hannibal and his elephants used daily for a month.

I recall finding one such saddle that was the only easy route between two canyons for several miles along the divide that separated them. The one trail that actually crossed the pass was several feet wide and churned up with deer tracks, leaving no doubt that it was used a great deal. It handled so much traffic that taking a stand for muleys at that spot seemed to make sense, although sitting and waiting for mule deer is a pretty iffy tactic. I did wait; it was a long wait, but muleys finally showed up. They used the trail with the assurance of critters walking up the path to their front door.

When scouting the approaches to saddles and passes, you will find that numerous trails lead into and away from one "mother" trail within the saddle itself. So saddles can be good starting points from which to launch off on trails that can take you in a number of different directions.

There are times, however, when the saddle trail itself may be particularly productive. Where one canyon that receives heavy hunting pressure parallels another canyon that gets hunted lightly, mule deer in search of refuge from all the commotion may use saddle trails heavily during the first week of the season.

Saddles also get frequent use right after the first heavy snow of autumn. It is not unusual for mule deer that summer on one side of a divide to use winter ranges on the other side. And it's the first good snow of the year that sets them in motion toward winter range. Your chances of catching them when they actually go over the pass may be fairly slim, but from the saddle, deer will fan out on the trails that descend toward winter range. They will congregate above this area until winter really sets in, so these tributary trails are good places to hunt.

Finally, there are the local mule deer that may use saddle trails on a daily basis. The side of a divide that has a north or east aspect is likely to be used more often during the day be-

Even in broken country, deer often utilize familiar travel routes. Finding those routes can lead to greater success for hunters. (Rodney Schlecht)

cause it will have thicker escape cover. The south or west side of a divide, on the other hand, may be used more at night because it is often sparsely vegetated. Local deer that are taking advantage of saddles to provide access to these different parts of their habitat will naturally use saddle trails in the evening and morning. This is the time to be there to stand- or still-hunt.

RIDGES AND CANYONS

Trails that meander back along the divides or up through the canyon bottoms are formed by mule deer on their way to greener pastures. These are migration routes, and they can go for miles into the backcountry. I've used them to get into little-used fishing spots and up to good elk country, but primarily for mule deer hunting.

Ridge and canyon trails may not always be right on the backbone of ridges or directly in canyon bottoms. More often they are broken trails running parallel to, but below, ridgetops and above canyon bottoms. They rarely make a beeline for anywhere. They're rather haphazard in their direction, but when you stay with them they work back into less heavily hunted country where large bucks are prone to stay.

One fall I was still-hunting on a game trail close to a ridge at about 7,500 feet. A movement just behind a steep shoulder brought me up short. As I waited I could hear leaves being rustled about and twigs snapping. The soft duff of the game trail had allowed me to move in close to whatever was back there without being detected. For a while I thought the animal was moving away, but then the scuffling sounds grew louder, and a mule deer head adorned with many points poked into view.

That's the kind of apparition that puts the proof into game-trail hunting for mule deer.

HUNTING
MIGRATORY MULEYS

"Mule deer go up in the summer and come down in the winter." That's about as far as many of us get when describing muley migrations—movements that usually take place in the middle of hunting season and greatly affect where hunters should go.

But the real situation is much more complicated. Depending on the habitat, mule deer may migrate in unexpected patterns, spurred by heat or cold, drought or snow. You may find them moving down in the fall or you may find them moving up. You may even find them moving up in order to move down.

Whether you're hunting mule deer in forested mountain terrain, out on the prairies, or down in the breaks (river drainages), you will find muleys using unique migratory strategies that are governed by the weather. I've touched on these patterns throughout this book, but let's take a more detailed approach—much of your hunting success depends on knowing where and why migrating deer move.

PRAIRIES

We don't usually think of the prairie as a place where mule deer migrate. In some areas, however, they may move as much as fifty miles between summer and winter grounds, although four to six miles is more common.

By mid-October in these open areas, sun, heat, and a lack of rain have usually dried up most vegetation on the sagebrush grasslands, and the deer have begun their migration by moving onto the northern sides of slopes and ridges where shaded areas in hardwood draws still hold some succulent forage.

This initial move—one that takes the deer uphill—may only mean a change in location of a few miles, but if you're still wandering around in the sagebrush where you saw deer in August, you might as well be 100 miles away.

The north slopes and their draws represent the fall transition lands for prairie mule deer, as long as real winter weather stays away. Since these gathering spots do not represent a large percentage of the area of the Great Plains, the number of deer congregated there may surprise you.

North slopes offer good places to use drive tactics, with one person walking up the center of a draw and several others posted ahead along either side where they have a good view into the bottoms. I have even had success sitting at a good overlook for an hour or two at first light or at dusk.

At some point during the hunting season winter weather is likely to set in. At this time a migration that was initiated by heat and drought is spurred to completion by cold and snow, and again the move is upward.

This upward migration might seem strange until you consider the geography of the plains. Much of the erosion evident on a prairie takes place on the hills and buttes, since they are suscep-

Hunters who aren't used to chasing mule deer on the prairies may be surprised to find that deer move "up" to the badlands as winter weather moves in. (Rodney Schlecht)

tible to the run-off of rain and melting snow. What results is a collection of gullies and cuts running every which way through the higher ground that forms the high-country badlands. For deer this area offers both shelter and food in the face of winter weather.

Because of the varied shapes of the ridges and draws, there is always somewhere for deer to find shelter from the wind, which is almost always blowing on the prairie. In addition, most of the snow drifts along the periphery of the badlands, leaving the middle fairly snow-free for deer to move about in.

Looking at the amount of food available in these highlands, you may wonder why muleys gather there. The vegetation that does grow in these areas in extremely diverse because of the different microclimates typical of a landscape that faces in many directions. Not only is there a wide variety of food, but the plants also remain edible longer—even late into the fall— because the vegetation catches the autumn rain and is protected from the sun and heat.

Once cold, snowy weather has begun on the plains, these badlands become home for the mule deer, and hunting them is best done by systematically walking the edges of eroded fingers of land that jut into their center.

BREAKS

Throughout mule deer territory in the West, there are numerous rivers of considerable size. They have not only burrowed down into the land, but their tributary streams and even intermittent drainage sites have also eroded the terrain, often for five or six miles back from the floodplains.

At the farthest points from the rivers, these drainages are only shallow indentations, but as they get closer to the rivers, they become deeper, sometimes cutting down hundreds of feet by the time they reach the floodplains.

During the summer mule deer can find plenty of food and room in the tops of river drainages, miles away from the rivers. When vegetation starts to dry out in the fall, however, muleys begin to move down toward the rivers. In deepening coulees and draws, the deer find moisture, shade, and green vegetation. They linger in these transition areas just as prairie muleys may stay for days or weeks on north-slope hillsides and ridges.

Because muleys are very traditional in their use of home ranges, they usually return to the same one or two draws each year. So hunting in familiar breaks can be a frustrating hit-or-miss proposition at times. However, once you do find a coulee being used by deer, you can count on that spot being productive year after year.

Hunt the midsections of these ravines the same way you'd hunt north-slope hardwood draws in their prairie habitat; that is, walk down through their bottoms or take a stand along their edges at dawn and dusk.

With the arrival of more winter-like weather in the fall, the muleys descend farther into the breaks until they reach the maze of deep coulees close to the river. This is where forage is sparse but diverse, and it's where deer find protection from wind and snow.

Since the walls of these coulees may reach up for hundreds of feet, you have to get right down in them to hunt effectively. And like the shallower ravines farther back from the rivers, you may find some areas curiously deerless. Keep trying different coulees until you are successful.

MOUNTAINS AND FOOTHILLS

Mountains and foothills are usually the habitat that hunters think about when it comes to mule deer migration—but even here some strange patterns of movement can occur.

Unlike the other areas where heat and drought get them going, muleys at high elevation start to head for lower ground with the arrival of cold and snow. But some muleys, summering high up on one side of a mountain range, may have a traditional wintering area on the opposite side of the mountains. So instead of just moving downhill, they must go up and over the divide before they travel down.

Once, having glassed out a pocket of bucks in the high country at the beginning of the season, I decided I had them cornered. All I had to do was wait for a good storm and they'd be pushed down lower in the drainage where I could hunt

In mountain/foothills habitat, the traditional mule deer migration is to a lower elevation, although many herds actually migrate up and over divides to reach winter range on the other side. (David Heffernan/USFWS)

them easily. The storm came, but the bucks disappeared. Later, I happened to talk with a wildlife biologist who'd spent years monitoring their movements. Those deer never did come down my side of the mountain; they went over the top to reach their winter range on the other side.

But even in the mountains the deer don't always go directly to their wintering grounds on the lower, open foothills. Instead, they descend only partway to the forested midsections of the mountains and congregate in a band *above* their winter range. This is where you should look for muleys as winter weather intensifies.

Since cold weather forces the deer to migrate to areas of low security down on open foothills, muleys may not actually move onto their winter range until after the hunting season, preferring to stay within the protection of the forest as long as possible. (I'll have more to say on these "holding patterns" of mountain/foothill muleys in the next chapter.)

Perhaps the most important thing to remember about hunting migratory mule deer in any habitat is that their movements are going to be determined by weather. For example, if there is a cool, moist summer on the prairie, the deer are not going to move up onto north slopes as early as they would at the end of a hot, dry summer. Or if summer-like weather lingers into the fall in the mountains, mule deer will remain in the high country longer and filter downward slowly. On the other hand, a hard winter storm can send them from summer range to winter range overnight, even if it means moving a dozen miles.

Going after migratory mules is more than just thinking about up and down. Landscape and weather are necessary considerations if you want to be where the deer are.

HOLDING PATTERNS

In any place where there are migratory mule deer, hunters tend to focus their attention on muley summer range before harsh weather hits and on muley winter range after it hits. Some hunters try to catch mule deer during the short period in which the deer are moving between summer and winter ranges. But only a few hunters target mule deer "holding areas" because only a few hunters know they exist.

Holding areas are specific pieces of terrain that muleys use to satisfy their needs when they either can't or don't want to use their usual seasonal home ranges. Autumn holding areas are obviously of special interest to hunters. Like summer and winter ranges, holding areas are traditional areas of use. Younger deer learn the location of holding areas by following older deer, and this knowledge is passed on from generation to generation. So when cold weather and deep snow prompt deer to move off their summer range, they don't simply move to any lower elevation area that offers tolerable conditions. They move swiftly and directly to a specific holding area they have learned to use in the past.

In mountain habitats, part of the muley population goes on the move toward winter range at the first sign of winter. These are the deer that summer on one side of a mountain

range and winter on the other. They occur in surprising numbers in any mountain mule deer population.

The early move toward winter range is designed to get
deer over mountain passes before snow closes them in. But
once over the divide the deer tend to bunch up in holding
areas where they may spend the entire hunting season before
finally moving to traditional winter range later on.

The initial movement over mountain divides to a holding
area is prompted not by weather conditions on summer range,
but on conditions at the divide itself or conditions at a saddle
or pass used to get over the divide. Consequently, divide-crossing deer may move to holding areas at the first dusting of snow
on the highest peaks, which may happen before the hunting
season even opens.

Although divide-crossing deer are the first deer to move to
holding areas, all muleys using high-elevation summer ranges—
and these are often bucks—are very sensitive to weather change
and will move to holding areas soon after the divide-crossers if
snow starts to accumulate on their summer range.

The amount of time deer spend in autumn holding areas
may range from several weeks to several months, but they seem
to hold there for as long as the weather permits. The motiva-
tion for this may be to avoid concentrating in large numbers
on winter range where competition for forage is high, along
with danger from predators. Deer also stay in holding areas to
avoid hunting pressure. Such areas are located at elevations
midway between summer and winter ranges, but they tend to
be in closer proximity to winter range, usually within a half-
mile to three miles.

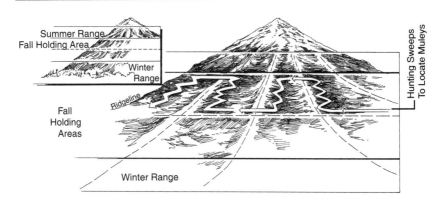

Snow doesn't always move muleys — at least not as far as you'd think. Before you rush to their winter range, visit the area just below their summer range.

With weather moving deer down from above and hunting pressure pushing them up from below, mule deer concentrations in autumn holding areas occur in bands within mid-elevation forests. The harsher the weather and the greater the hunting pressure, the narrower these bands of deer densities become.

Strangely, west-slope holding areas are the first to fill up in the fall. The reason for this probably stems from the earliest colonization of mountain/foothill areas by mule deer. The drier east slopes of mountain ranges — influenced by the "rain shadow" effect — offer better conditions for year-round deer habitation in one location. So these areas were probably colonized first because they didn't require deer to migrate between summer and winter ranges or because they required only a short migration.

As deer populations grew on the east slopes, however, emigrating offspring were forced to the wetter, snowier west slopes where survival strategies grew complicated, including — as population pressure increased even here — crossing the divide to find suitable unclaimed summer range. As a result, most divide-crossing muleys have holding areas and winter ranges on the west slopes and summer ranges on the east slopes.

Scouting for either west-slope or east-slope holding areas should start by identifying winter ranges located along open foothills. There may be two or three separate winter ranges along each side of a mountain range, and each one will have a holding area located above it. South and southwest slopes are likely winter range spots since they will hold the least snow.

Winter scouting trips conducted by car, snowmobile, or ski can reveal the locations of winter ranges simply by the obvious concentrations of deer in these areas after a snow. But summer scouting can also be effective, even though deer may not be in the vicinity.

Not long ago I was visiting a friend in Idaho during the summer, and we were bushwhacking down from some mountain lakes where we'd been catching and releasing hefty 16-inch cutthroats. (The fish in those lakes had not always been so cooperative, let me assure you.) After breaking out of the forest, we were treated to a view of the hay-meadowed valley below. We stopped there to admire the scenery and uncap our water bottles.

The longer we sat there, the more I began to take in the sights closer at hand. I noticed juniper and sagebrush with new growth bristling out of stubby and clubbed woody branches. On the ground, what I first thought to be pebbles turned out to be deer droppings. The hillside was covered with them. Though there wasn't a deer in sight, I knew we were sitting in the heart of a mule deer winter range. Above that spot, I found one of the best muley holding areas I've ever hunted.

Heavily browsed bushes on any winter range will always have a stunted and clubbed appearance, with occasional new growth sprouting out of a fist-like knob of woody branches. This, along with lots of droppings, is the first thing to look for when scouting for winter range.

If it's not possible to scout out these winter ranges on your own (when you've only got a week or so to hunt unfamiliar territory, for example), you'll have to rely on local advice. Most anyone who knows the whereabouts of winter mule deer ranges is willing to point them out because doing so doesn't appear to give away the location of any local hunting hotspots. Sporting goods stores are good places to start your inquiries.

Regional fish and game headquarters are other sources to check. Many of these agencies will have mule deer winter ranges identified on maps or will be able to point out where such ranges exist.

When these sources fail, a large-scale topographic map purchased in a local sporting goods store can reveal a great deal. Look for open south and southwest ridges that poke out farther into a valley than adjacent ridges. If there are any mule deer in the area at all, these particular ridges are likely to serve as their wintering groups. Holding areas, the spots where mule deer are most likely to be concentrated during the hunting season, will be located in mid-elevation forests above these ranges.

You should remember that movement to holding areas is weather-dependent. First snows almost anywhere along the divide will start the divide-crossers in motion. Subsequent snows that begin to accumulate on high-elevation summer ranges

Knowing the routes mule deer take to reach their winter range will allow you to intercept them when the weather turns bad. (Rodney Schlecht)

will set other deer off to their holding areas. Therefore, you can catch muleys on the move if the mountains are free of snow before the season starts and you are attuned to upcoming storms.

Several factors work in your favor. Any mountain pass or saddle that gives easy access across a divide will almost always get considerable mule deer traffic during or right after the first several snows of the season. The fewer the passes along a divide, the more deer traffic they will get.

If your timing is right, you won't have to sit for days waiting for deer to cross over these traditional travel routes. Tracking studies have shown that once muleys make up their minds to move to holding areas, they can cover up to fifteen miles in as many hours. Figuring that the typical distance between summer range and autumn holding areas is much less than that, you may only have to wait a few hours after a storm sets in before you get deer activity in mountain saddles.

One particular mule deer hunting season that started with record-breaking warm temperatures ended, for me, in just such a mountain pass with snow swirling in great eddies through the trees. For over a week every hunter I knew had been moaning about the weather and the absence of deer. And for over a week I'd been tuned to my weather channel radio. It was on a Wednesday that I heard the news. A deep low-pressure system was approaching the state and was expected to bring up to a foot of new snow by Thursday night.

Thursday morning, with the barometer diving, I headed on foot for a saddle that was within two miles of a major mule deer winter range. By late morning I was posted along a well-worn game trail, and three hours later, with snow already blanketing their backs, muleys were crossing the divide. A broad-beamed four-pointer was among them.

Catching muleys on the move as they make a once-a-season trip over mountain passes is an iffy proposition, though, and a short-term hunting situation at best. The holding areas themselves are the spots on which to focus your attention for most of the season.

By making sweeps up one ridge and down another midway between open foothills and timberline, you should begin to locate concentrations of mule deer. Note the relative elevations at which you begin to see the deer so you can further narrow your hunting focus.

Within these areas of focus, bucks will look for different terrain than does, unless the rut is on. Segregated from does until breeding starts, bucks typically inhabit what most hunters view as inferior habitat. They hang out at higher elevations in forested holding areas where snow accumulation is deeper. Bucks may also be found in more rocky, rugged terrain where forage isn't as plentiful or as readily available.

As you zigzag through bands of autumn holding areas, look for these islands of more marginal habitat and return to them often. Also remember that holding areas will get narrower as weather and hunting pressure intensify. This means muley concentrations will become greater.

On one particularly memorable occasion, I watched while some hunters tromped through the woods below an autumn holding area and a few others marched right on through it to the rugged high country above, leaving me and a few hunting companions alone with a whole bunch of muleys on hold. That was quite a day.

MULE DEER IN ANY WEATHER

The wind was impossible. It whipped through branches of fir and lodgepole, sending great clumps of snow thumping to the ground. Tree trunks creaked and groaned under the strain, and miniature ground blizzards blew around my knees.

It was no day to be hunting, I thought, as I peered into the third deerless draw that funneled wind down through the forest. Where numerous mule deer had been the day before, now there were only flailing branches. Discouraged, I decided to follow the draw to where I knew it opened onto a series of wide terraces. There I could hit a wood road that would take me home to fire's warmth and hot coffee.

But as I walked onto the first of those terraces, changes began to occur. The wind died down and with it the noise and the movement of trees and snow. Just as I stood marveling at the calm, a doe and her fawn moved from behind a young lodgepole. Farther down the wood road, two more muleys appeared, and then a group of four. By the time I'd crossed the terraces and was breaking out onto the windy meadow beyond, I'd seen thirteen mule deer within an area of about fifteen acres. The deer had obviously found a niche in their range where there was relief from the worst of the weather.

Of course, it's common knowledge that mule deer are influenced by the weather. High wind makes muleys nervous. And mule deer tend to eat heartily after a storm. Only recently, however, has the full importance of weather on mule deer behavior been recognized.

Heat and cold, rain and snow, wind and barometric pressure, skies cloudy and clear all have their particular influence on where mule deer go to eat and rest and how and when they move. And research suggested that localized weather niches, or microclimates, are extremely important in attracting mule deer concentrations when weather conditions are unpleasant.

Since most of us don't have the luxury of being able to wait for "perfect" hunting days, we have to take the weather as it comes on the days we can hunt. So knowing how weather affects mule deer behavior is an important element in planning where and how to hunt.

Perhaps the most basic rule is this: Every move a mule deer makes in harsh weather is calculated to minimize energy drain and maximize energy gain. The deer will avoid climatic extremes whenever possible, and finding favorable microclimates may become more important than finding abundant food supplies.

The case of windy weather is a good example of the importance of finding microclimates because it occurs so frequently during the fall hunting season throughout the West. Wind in mild weather will compromise a deer's security, since he'll have difficulty hearing and smelling danger. In cold weather, both his security *and* his comfort are compromised. In either case, he'll head for areas that offer some protection. On the prairie he'll look for rough breaks or the thick brush of

Find a place where the terrain provides a respite from strong wind and you'll often find mule deer. (Rodney Schlecht)

creek bottoms. In the forest, he'll go into thick timber on north slopes. If these larger areas of protection are lacking, he'll find a depression in the ground, the lee of an uprooted tree, or a boulder to break the wind. And given particularly windy conditions, he may stay bedded until the wind dies down.

A friend recently encountered such wind conditions while hunting in south-central Montana. "It was one of the windiest days I've ever hunted in the Ponderosa country," Dave said. "There were literally no deer up and moving. And all I was doing was just working into the wind and peeking over little hills and peeking around rocks. I must have seen fifteen deer that day. Most of them were in their beds, or they had just stood up and were trying to figure out what I was."

Windy weather is just one instance where muleys will seek very localized niches in their environment to provide protection. Snow conditions also push into these microclimates. While snow is actually falling, deer tend to bed down where the lay of the land offers protection from blowing snow and where a canopy of vegetation offers protection from falling snow. In a forest habitat, such niches are regularly found in the lee of hills and ridges, and under thickly crowned stands of timber.

I came upon such a spot one fall while hunting a north-south divide. A snowstorm had blown in from the west and was making life miserable on that side of the ridge. Seeking a protected place to eat a sandwich, I topped the divide and dropped into another world. Not 100 feet below the ridgeline I sat in relative calm while watching treetops being whipped into a frenzy above me. As I ate, I discovered where the deer had come—a set of ears here, a rump patch there. A storm raged only a few feet away, but here snow just slowly sifted down through the evergreen ceiling. I started looking for the big buck that might have sought refuge there.

A storm like this on the prairie would send muleys into those wide, steep-sided draws where drifts pile up on the tops of the draw but leave the brushy bottoms fairly free of snow. Shallow, narrow draws that lie across the path of the blowing snow are rarely used by deer because they collect snow easily.

The condition of snow on the ground—long after it has stopped falling—will also influence mule deer. As a general rule, they will gravitate to areas where snow cover is shallowest and softest. According to researchers, mule deer will "expend four to five times as much energy walking in sixteen inches of snow, and seven to eight times as much energy in twenty inches of snow, as walking on bare ground."

Especially after the first snows of the season, deer will seek lower snow depths under the canopy of thick conifer forests, and they will feed where wind has blown snow away from the lee of fallen tree roots and from around stumps and tree trunks. I've seen track concentrations—and many a mule deer—around these spots after early season snowfalls. However, as snow depths increase, even under the protection of the forest, deer shift their feeding to open south slopes where the sun has a chance to melt the snow and where browse is more readily available.

Crusty snow is particularly hard on deer even at shallow depths. They can't paw through it to get at buried forage, and it provides unstable footing that can cut their legs. Avoiding crusty snow conditions is often a matter of timing, not a matter of changing locations.

A number of years ago, early season snowfalls followed by a succession of warm days and cold nights made for very crunchy morning snow conditions—the kind where you wince at each step you take and wonder why you didn't stay at home in bed. I had seen no deer moving for several mornings even though I was out at first light, and I assumed their absence was due to the noise I was making. It wasn't until other commitments forced me to hunt in the afternoon that I discovered what seemed to be happening.

The deer, it appeared, were staying bedded well into the day to avoid the crusty conditions I'd been nosing around in every morning. But by noon or early afternoon the temperatures had risen enough to soften the snow considerably. So afternoon became the peak time for deer movement. It was the peak time for me to move, too.

While snow in the air—and on the ground, under certain conditions—tends to keep muleys in protected beds longer than normal, the periods just before and just after a snowstorm are generally times of great deer activity. Although there has been no definite link established between atmospheric pressure and deer movement, researchers have noted increased deer activity before major storms and have attributed this to the presence of low atmospheric pressure. It seems to be a time to fill the belly before having to lie low. Once the skies clear, there is another burst of feeding activity to replenish empty stomachs. It's this calm after the storm that I've found to be the most productive weather for hunting mule deer.

But there are calms and there are *cold* calms. And temperatures at either cold or hot extremes will greatly influence where and when muleys congregate. Cold, however, is the most likely extreme during the hunting season in most mule deer habitat.

I recall one prolonged snowfall that stopped shortly after dark. By the time I was ready for bed the skies were clear and an almost full moon reflected from every snow crystal as the mercury in the thermometer outside my kitchen window began to sink. How far it would drop, I didn't know. But, considering the three days it had snowed, I was pretty sure the full moon would see deer feeding out in the open for the rest of the night and I would find them there at daylight.

At 6 A.M., the thermometer read minus fifteen degrees Fahrenheit. I was not thrilled about going out in that, no matter what the hunting prospects, but I did. And there were no deer out in the open where they were supposed to be. There weren't even any tracks out in the open.

Following the law of minimizing energy drain and maximizing energy gain, the deer had remained under the protection of the conifers, which served as a shield against radiant heat loss. That's where I finally found them, munching on the tops of exposed huckleberry bushes. Had I waited until the sun had warmed those open slopes, I would have found them where I thought they should have been earlier. I still would have had a successful morning of hunting, and I'd have been a lot warmer in the process.

Muleys are also sensitive to less dramatic temperatures. In cold weather, they'd prefer to bed down in a ridgeside spot of sun rather than a chilly pocket of frost. And when temperature inversions come in, as they frequently do along the Rockies, you can bet the deer are going to gravitate to the warmer temperatures of the higher slopes, as long as snow conditions permit.

Temperature is often connected to cloud cover, and this is another aspect of weather to consider when trying to figure out how current weather conditions might affect mule deer hunting.

Muleys usually stay put during heavy snowstorms, but they may become active just before or after a storm. (Rodney Schlecht)

In both warm and cold weather, cloud cover moderates temperatures, making them warmer when it's cold and cooler when it's hot. These moderating effects tend to extend the morning feeding activity and prompt an earlier start to afternoon feeding.

What seems to most influence mule deer, however, is a major contrast to a prevailing weather pattern. For example, by the first part of October muleys along the Rockies are in their winter pelage (heavier winter coat). Their metabolism has adjusted to cooler weather, and their bodies are generally ready for the onset of winter. So if a warm stretch of Indian summer comes in at the end of October, sending temperatures up into the high sixties, the deer are really going to feel it. The same temperatures in July would hardly be noticed, but in the fall this heat will send muleys for the shade and dampness of north-slope timber or for brushy creek bottoms where running water offers some cooling effect.

Several years ago, a different sort of weather contrast finally brought some successful hunting to an otherwise difficult season. For weeks, the days had been beautiful, the kind of clear skies and brisk temperatures that are ideal for late-season trout fishing, raking leaves, flying kites with the kids—anything but mule deer hunting.

Then, at the start of the second week in November, a deep low-pressure trough swept over the region, followed by a big, steady storm that dumped a foot of snow overnight. By morning it was over.

The sudden and dramatic change in the weather had caught the deer by surprise. They were being forced to seek lower ground. They were also being forced to find niches in the lower ground where forage, warmth, and cover were most readily available. Suddenly their open range had become very restricted because of the weather.

Successful hunting under these and other varied weather conditions requires a sense of where mule deer will find protection, where the lay of the land and the forest and thickets will provide relief from the heat or the cold, the wind or the snow. You'll have a better feel for these areas in country with which you are familiar. But even in new territory, you can make educated guesses about mule deer whereabouts under any weather conditions if you remember that they're always trying to expend the least, and conserve the most, energy possible.

As one wildlife biologist friend puts it, "Muleys are probably going to go where any good woodsman would go to find relief and protection from the weather at hand."

BUCKS IN RUT

When hunting new territory, I've found it takes some time to get the feel of how game uses the area. That certainly was the case when I moved from the rolling hills of New England to the mountain country of Montana. I remember best the learning process I had to go through while trying to locate mule deer in the Rockies, especially muleys in rut; my first few seasons in Montana really put my patience to a test. Mule deer bucks didn't seem to exist. I eventually shot a big doe at the edge of a forest one morning after seeing nothing but does and fawns during my many days afield.

I began to concentrate on elk. All the locals told me I'd have to hunt high, and that's just what I did. But to my surprise, in addition to finding elk in the natural parklands below the divide where I hunted, mule deer also appeared. In the course of a week, I saw three good-sized bucks.

This happened during the first week in November. But for the rest of the season, the responsibilities of a new job limited my hunting to weekends. On those days, I continued to hunt the snowy high country for elk, while keeping a curious eye out for the muley bucks. I never saw them again.

What I did see while driving to work early in the mornings during the second week in November, however, just added to my confusion. On two different occasions, two different mule deer bucks appeared near the road along the edge of fields bordered by fir forests. But after that week, I didn't see another buck or doe until well into December, long after hunting season had ended.

I didn't know what to make of it. For the first half of the season, I hadn't seen any bucks in the heartland of the forest. Yet I had seen some up high, before the snows came in early November. Then they seemed to disappear. I'd also seen some bucks down low until about the middle of November. Then they, too, seemed to vanish.

The next season I was determined to find a trophy buck, so I devised a plan. First, I would concentrate my efforts high up along the alpine meadows and down along the forest edges because these were the places I'd actually seen mule deer bucks the year before. Second, to tip the scale even more in my favor, I planned to hunt during the rut, since the bucks would be distracted and easier to move in on at that time.

I'd heard that the rut started around mid-November in the area I planned to hunt, so I concentrated on bird hunting until that time. Then, for the last two weeks of the season, I put all my efforts into finding a big mule deer. I hunted high and I hunted low, but I still came up empty. I was completely mystified. Oh, I'd seen a few deer, and even some young bucks, but no wall-hangers.

It wasn't until I had a talk with wildlife biologist Dave Pac that I could make any sense of those first two years of hunting muleys in the Rockies. I learned that mule deer in the mountain-foothill habitats have a sandwiched social structure throughout the summer and early fall. Mature bucks occupy

When the rut is on, mule deer bucks cover a lot of ground in search of does.

the outer edges of this range—the forest edges up along the divides and down along agricultural land and sagebrush slopes. Does, fawns, and young bucks, on the other hand, congregate in the forested mid-elevations.

This explained what I'd observed during the first part of my first year of Western hunting, but it didn't explain why the bucks weren't in those high and low areas at the end of the season, during the rut. The explanation I got from Pac had that obvious kind of simplicity that made me feel dumb. The bucks, of course, had moved to where the does were, those vast forested middle elevations where I'd hunted earlier, before the bucks had moved in.

Since that time, Pac has taught me some other things about muleys in rut. And I have discovered that the normal mule deer movements, behavior patterns, and dispositions that

251

exist during the rest of the year are generally disrupted when these deer are mating.

When they mate is a matter of latitude. Research has discovered that the relationship between daylight hours and nighttime hours—a relationship called photoperiodism—is responsible for triggering rut. In Montana, for example, the rut usually gets underway around November 10, peaks about November 25, and ends around December 15. However, as you move south, where daylight hours remain longer later in the year, the rut will not start until later in the fall. This variation in the timing of the rut is important to recognize and check on when planning a hunting trip to areas with which you are unfamiliar.

Once the rut does begin, deer movement increases—especially buck movement. According to Pac, "There's data that show during rut there is a decrease in bedding time and feeding time, and a gross increase in distance traveled—at least time up and moving. There's also an increase in overall home-range size. The bucks just start moving out and covering a lot of ground.

"During the rut, when things are really peaked out, they'll be moving all day long. The idea that deer are most active during morning and evening doesn't really apply at this time. You'll see them wandering around following doe trails with their noses on the ground, looking like bloodhounds."

The bloodhound comparison is apt. After hunting muleys in the West for almost two decades now, I've seen this head-down, headlong pursuit of does on numerous occasions. During one late fall I was hunting a particular forested draw that I knew to be a favorite doe hangout. After still-hunting there for about half an hour, I saw a doe come fidgeting through the trees on the ridge. Earlier in the season, I wouldn't have paid much attention to her presence. But it was mid-November, so I sat down in the snow and waited. Within two or three minutes, another deer moved along the ridge. Its nose-to-the-ground posture was a sure giveaway, but I waited until I saw antlers before raising my rifle.

Monitoring of bucks during rut has shown that they regularly check doe gathering areas. So it makes sense to pinpoint these spots earlier in the year, although bucks won't be there at that time. In areas I hunt regularly, I've found several spots where does routinely congregate, spots they use year after year.

One thing that will drive deer away from their usual hangouts is snow and cold. In the area where I usually hunt mule deer, the average elevation range where I'll find does—and therefore bucks—during the rut is between 6,500 and 8,000 feet. But several seasons ago, a particularly harsh fall storm dumped a lot of snow and sent the thermometer down near zero. At 7,500 feet along a local divide, I was plowing through knee-deep snow with no sign of does, so I dropped down to 7,000 feet. Still no deer—even in areas I knew to be some of their favorite haunts. It wasn't until I'd dropped down to nearly 6,500 feet that I started seeing deer. And there, in a narrow band of timber just above the open sagebrush slopes, I really got into them, thanks to a squeeze play brought on by the weather.

Once you do locate the does and the bucks during rut, you'll often find the bucks behaving in a way that has been characterized as "lovesick."

"Bucks in rut are very noisy," says Pac. "They're very un-concerned. They make lots of mistakes, just blundering around with their minds on one thing. They're not monitoring their surroundings like they are in other seasons. They're not eating; they're not sleeping. They're not being cautious, in most cases. Sometimes, they're dumber than fenceposts. You know these big, prime-age bucks that are supposed to be so smart? Sometimes they literally just walk right up to you."

Pac is quick to admit, however, that this is not always the case. And Canadian researcher Valerius Geist even suggests that it is to a buck's advantage to be inconspicuous during rut so as not to attract competitors. Does, on the other hand, have an ad-vantage in being conspicuous in order to attract dominant males.

There is no doubt that competition does exist at this time, though. Before the peak of the rut, bucks of unequal size spar with one another after beating the brush with their horns. These sparring matches can be noisy and lengthy, but rarely bloody; they may be helpful in attracting you, but they rarely attract other bucks. Their main purpose appears to be a display of dominance by the larger male who instigates such bouts.

True dominance fights, however, are as serious as they are rare. When they occur, they take place at the peak of the rut between two mature bucks of equal size. And they tend to be very short. I have never witnessed a dominance fight, and nei-ther has Pac, who has spent more hours observing mule deer than most serious hunters.

The rareness of dominance fights among muley bucks is one reason why rattling up bucks as a hunting technique for this species isn't very effective. The mule deer temperament just isn't as volatile as that of the whitetail, for which rattling is a more successful tool.

Deer density also has a lot to do with the success of rattling. According to Pac, "If you're in a situation where there's a high density of whitetail bucks, there's probably a high density of male-to-male interaction and a lot of chance for two equally matched bucks to meet up. And they're going to settle it with a fight.

"Texas, for example, has some hellacious whitetail densities where a guy's chances of sitting down in a brush patch and being within ear shot of a dozen different bucks is pretty good."

Fights like this one are a rare sight among mule deer, which is one reason why rattling isn't a great technique for bucks in rut. (Rodney Schlecht)

The lack of this kind of density in most mule deer habitats is another reason most hunters have found rattling an ineffective technique.

The lack of population density and the level-headed temperament of the mule deer is probably also responsible for the relative ineffectiveness of deer calls for muleys. Although muley bucks do make a soft, low-pitched imitation of a fawn's alarm sound to attract does during rut, it rarely attracts other bucks. And though some hunters have had luck in calling black-tailed deer in Oregon, success with mule deer has been limited, despite the enthusiasm a few hunters have for this technique.

Basically, then, the key elements of a successful hunt for mule deer in rut are their mobility and their traditional use of certain areas.

"When you're hunting mule deer outside the rut, the mobility of bucks is probably very low," says Pac, "lower than normal at that time of year because they're aware of hunting disturbance, and they're focusing all their attention on you the hunter. That means that you've got to cover a lot more distance to increase your chances of jumping a buck. So it's a totally different strategy than during rut.

"The increased movement of bucks during rut is a great advantage to the hunter in that, if he goes into an area where there are bucks in rut, and he moves very slowly with the wind in his favor, those bucks are going to bump into him. That's been my experience. Use that buck movement in your favor. Don't try to cover a lot of ground at that time of year; the buck is already covering it. You just intercept him."

Though Pac advocates hunting extremely slowly during the rut, he does not suggest taking a stand. "For mule deer, in my experience, stand-hunting isn't nearly as dependable as it is for whitetails for the simple reason that muleys are not as traditional in using a given trail system. But they are traditional in the use of a particular area."

This traditional use of an area is important to key in on. Certainly, the weather has a great deal to do with where you'll find deer concentrations during rut. The more cold and snow you have, the closer the deer will be to their winter range on southern and western foothills. But even with restrictions placed on them by the weather, muleys have favorite areas where they gather, leaving other areas at the same elevation deerless.

In most cases, I've found mule deer during the rut under fairly sparse forest canopies on southern slopes with reasonably close access to thicker timber. This usually means they'll be in areas close to spur ridges or low divides where a quick dash over the top puts them on more heavily forested northern slopes.

As one rut-wise hunting acquaintance sums it up, "Once you get into these lovesick muleys, you want to move real slow. But you gotta find 'em first. A fella looks kinda stupid sneakin' around in a piece of empty forest."

Planning Your Mule Deer Hunt

USING AN OUTFITTER OR GOING IT ALONE

O kay. You say you've hunted mule deer in the same place for years. You're ready for a change, a challenge, some new terrain. You want to go after muleys where you've never hunted them before, in some completely different part of your state, maybe in a different state or province altogether. Or perhaps you've never hunted muleys at all, and you're ready to give it a try. How do you go about putting a hunting trip together?

Above all, start your planning early. A year in advance of a trip is not too soon to begin asking lots of questions, doing research, and becoming well informed.

First, decide what you are looking for in a trip. Is going after a trophy or a big-antlered buck your main aim, or are you happy to just get a muley in some new terrain? What kind of habitat do you want to hunt? And what state are you interested in hunting?

You may know the answers to these questions from the outset, or your desires may change and evolve as you look into various possibilities and learn more about them. But before you get into the details of your planning, have a clear sense of your own expectations for the trip. And, if you are going on the trip with other hunters, make sure you all have similar goals, or goals that are at least compatible.

Once these basic expectations are clear, you'll have to decide whether to hire an outfitter or tackle the trip on your own. It's a big decision and an important one.

A GUIDED MULE DEER HUNT

A good guide will tell you when and where to apply for necessary licenses and permits and give you a complete list of the clothing and gear you'll need to bring. He'll know the idiosyncrasies of the local terrain, habitats, and game. He'll get you to the best places to hunt at the best times of day given the weather conditions. He'll feed you, wash your dishes, fix you a comfortable place to sleep, and wake you up when it's time to hunt. He'll tell you stories and listen to yours. He'll try all his tricks to get you hooked up with the kind of mule deer you want to shoot. And if you shoot it, he'll field dress the deer, pack it to camp, and ship it to your home or to the taxidermist.

A good guide will not guarantee that you'll shoot a trophy deer or even any deer. Getting a deer is just not a sure thing, even with the best of guides. You need to know that from the start.

A good guide will also charge you a good amount of money for his services. If you can't afford to pay for such a trip or you are unwilling to let go of that amount of cash, you're left to your own devices. That means you will have to be responsible for all the things a guide would do for you, in addition to hunting all day. You'll have to chop wood, cook meals, wash dishes, feed the fire all night, and keep the tent ropes tight. It can be done; it's just not quite as much fun for some hunters. Are you one of them?

While you're working toward making the guide or self-guide decision, there are some things you should check out on the Internet, which has become one of the best sources for getting up-to-date information for planning a hunting trip. If you don't have a computer with Internet access, most public libraries do. And if you are not familiar with computers, resource people at the library can help you use a search engine, such as Google or Jeeves, to find information.

Start your search by typing "state fish and game departments" into your search engine's search box. You'll quickly find a website that lists these departments alphabetically by state. Each state has its own lineup of trip-planning offerings, including mule deer seasons, rules and regulations, and the cost and due dates for resident and non-resident applications and permits. Most state and provincial fish and game websites provide a variety of other useful information, including such things as a list of private and public hunting opportunities, the status of state mule deer populations, big-game records, tips on planning a hunt, lists of outfitters and guides, and phone numbers where you can get more information if you have questions.

You can also ask Google or Jeeves or one of the other search engines to search for "mule deer hunts." That will bring up a list of outfitters who specialize in guided hunts for muleys in the U.S., Canada, and Mexico.

Perhaps the best place to get a feel for what outfitters have to offer, though, is a sportsmen's show where outfitters have booths and you can talk to them in person, ask questions, and get immediate responses.

Whether talking with an outfitter face to face or over the phone, here are some questions you might ask after you've explained what your hopes are for a hunt:

- How many years have you outfitted in your area?
- How many years will my guide have guided in the area?
- What kind of hunting will we be doing—vehicle, horse, foot, or combination?
- How many miles a day will we cover, over what kind of terrain?
- How long is the hunting day?
- How many days will we actually hunt?
- Will we be hunting on public or private land?
- What kind of accommodations and meals do you provide?
- How much horseback riding will I have to do on a pack trip into the backcountry?
- What is the total cost including extra fees, charges, permits, tips, etc.?
- Are there additional fees for a trophy or for shipping meat, hide, or antlers?
- What is your hunter-success ratio?
- Are you licensed and insured?
- Are you a member of the state outfitters and guides association?

Ask these questions of at least three outfitters who sound as though they could provide the services you're looking for.

Ask each outfitter for a list of references, including some hunters who didn't take any game. Call at least three references provided by each outfitter.

This will be time consuming, but when you're done, you'll have a clear idea of which outfitter will fill your needs the best, and you can sign on with him. Or you'll decide you can't afford the service, and you'll have to tackle the trip on your own.

SELF-GUIDED TRIP PLANNING

When planning for a self-guided trip, use the Internet resources I've mentioned above, plus any other leads you can find, to decide exactly where you want to hunt. Check out possibilities on both public and private land, and make sure hunting access is available to you. Then call state game managers in the areas you're considering to find out the status of the mule deer population, especially big bucks if you're interested in going for a trophy. (You can usually reach these game managers through information available on fish and game websites or by contacting regional fish and game offices within the state you plan to hunt.) Also make sure the kind of licenses you want are available for that hunting area.

Once you decide on a specific area, make all the necessary applications for licenses, permits, and tags well ahead of their due dates. Then purchase good topographic maps of the area, and use them to start to get a good mental picture of the lay of the land and how mule deer might use it.

Next, decide on hunting accommodations. A motel room will pamper you, but you'll have to drive to and from your hunting area each day. That could take valuable time out of the best hunting hours. A camp, on the other hand, will put you in or near the heart of good hunting, and that is usually preferable to the motel option.

If at all possible, make arrangements to secure a specific camp spot on private or public land, and confirm a reservation for that site. Find out what is provided at the site in the way of water, fire grates, tables, and so forth. Then determine what gear and equipment you'll need to bring to satisfy your expectations for a comfortable camp. Do you need a generator and a wall tent with a wood stove and a portable potty? Or can you be happy with a backpacker's tent and a flashlight?

When sharing the responsibility of providing camp gear and food with a group of hunters, use a master list to work from and to check off chores. Weeks before you depart on your hunting adventure, take a day to meet with all your hunting buddies with all your gear and provisions. Spread it all out, set it all up, make sure it all works. Check it off your master list. Then pack it up and make sure it fits in the vehicle you'll be taking. And be sure that vehicle is reliable, recently serviced, and sporting good tires. And, amid all this planning and equipping, figure out exactly how you will care for, process, store, and transport any game you get once you arrive at your mule deer hunting destination.

At this point you may be thinking that maybe you actually can afford the services of that outfitter who really did sound perfect for the hunt you want to take. So it might be appropriate to end this discussion, with a look at how some guides view their profession and the clients they serve.

Duaine Hagen, an outfitter out of Cody, Wyoming, has this to say about why he's in the guiding business: "It's the lifestyle. It sure beats sitting behind a desk. And the experience and enjoyment you provide your client is a big reward. I've got clients who live from year to year to come out here."

But Hagen will tell you that guiding has become more than just taking people hunting. "The role has changed for the outfitter and guide. We're not only expected to be good hunters and be able to get clients into game; we have to be naturalists, too. We have to interpret and we have to educate. And we're kind of responsible for the backcountry. So we teach low-impact camping techniques.

"In the past," says Hagen, "there were a lot of guides who had this macho thing where they were going to show the dude how tough they were. Well, those guys don't make it on my place very long. People are not coming out West to see how tough somebody else is. They're out here to have a good time and a good experience and to share it with somebody. It's our job to provide that."

In the process of doing so, guides meet a mixed bag of clients. Many of them make guides glad they're in the business, but some make for long days. These are the clients who don't want to pay attention to the rules, forcing the guide to double as game warden. They're the ones who can't be happy unless they shoot a trophy no matter what, or who expect to be shown a parade of muleys as if they were in a mule deer theme park, not the real forests, prairies, and deserts of the West.

But the rewards of guiding are strong, most outfitters agree. Outfitter Merritt Pride, of Montana's Lost Fork Outfitting and Guide School, likes to tell the story of a hunter from West Virginia who wanted to shoot a 30-inch typical four-point mule deer—a buck that Pride admitted would be hard to find.

On the first day, they went out and spotted a buck about 150 yards across a draw. "He was a super buck," Pride says. "He was probably 26 or 27 inches, big bodied. I mean, he was a hell of a deer. And Ed kept saying, 'Boy, he's nice,' and he asked me if I thought the buck was 30 inches."

Merritt didn't think so, and Ed didn't shoot. But they sat for an hour admiring the buck. And when they got back to their horses, Merritt asked Ed if he would have shot the deer had it been 30 inches.

"Probably not today," Ed said. "I came here to hunt."

Over the next six days, they saw 27 four-point bucks and never fired a shot. And in the end, Merritt told Ed he felt bad that he hadn't gotten him what he wanted.

"Oh, this is part of the fun," Ed said. "If I get that 30-inch buck, I'll just have to look for something else that's hard to find."

Ed is the kind of hunter that keeps Merritt Pride in the guiding profession. He is one of the big rewards.

DRESS FOR SUCCESS

Spotting a large mule deer buck casually feeding behind a small rise, Richard Thomas checked the wind, then crept to a hill directly above the deer. Once there, a branch of sagebrush met his nylon windbreaker with a loud pop. He topped the rise in time to see the back end of his buck disappear into the brush.

Elsewhere, Joe Richards rolled out of bed early to go deer hunting, still smelling of the cologne he'd worn the previous evening. At 11 A.M., the first and only deer to approach Joe's meticulously placed stand bolted before he ever raised his rifle.

Meanwhile, a small group of muleys lazed in a prairie basin, and Charlie Potter was sure there was a nice set of antlers in the bunch. But from his position on the ridge, grass blurred the image in his binoculars. Charlie rose ever so slowly to his knees, only to watch the deer quickly flee to the safety of a nearby ravine.

Although the names are fictitious, the events are real. They happen every day of the hunting season and are typical of the inattention given to the Three S's of hunting—Smells, Sounds, and Silhouettes. The Three S's are as basic to hunting big game as the Three R's are to grade school. Yet, a surprising

269

number of us fail to pay attention to these cornerstones when we choose our hunting clothing, and so we make hunting harder than it has to be.

SOUNDS

I once tested what was touted as the most advanced hunting suit to ever come along. It was waterproof without being stuffy; it was warm without being puffy, but it was the noisiest clothing I'd worn since retiring my Moose Bar bowling jacket. I sent the suit back to the manufacturer with appropriate comments.

The problem with many high-tech hunting materials used in clothing is that they have a very slick, hard finish. This makes them noisy when surfaces rub together or when they come against the stems and branches you inevitably encounter in the field.

At the risk of sounding like an old curmudgeon, I'd have to say that wool remains one of the best materials for sound-proofing your hunting wardrobe. It is still my choice for pants, jacket, gloves, and hat.

On the other hand, some synthetic materials are well suited for hunting apparel. Notable among these materials are nylon and polyester blends like fleece, pile, and hunter's cloth. Like wool, the materials are soft to the touch and quiet in the woods. But be forewarned, the fabrics with the real fuzzy feel have a magnetic attraction for all sort of burrs, twigs, and leaves. Hunting catalogs like Cabela's usually provide a wealth of clothing options for virtually any hunting situation, just make sure your hunting outfit performs the way you need it to before you wear it during hunting season.

The most offensive noisemaking item that hunters don each season, however, is the ubiquitous vinyl orange hunting vest. These go on sale before each opening day for a few dollars and you might as well wrap yourself in tinfoil for all the noise they make.

Years ago, when I was still doing some guiding, the wife of the outfitter I worked for presented all the guides with orange vests she had made from soft cotton cloth. I still use this vest today. Blaze orange cloth is available at most fabric stores, and a simple vest takes no time to put together. I suspect even I could do it. A variety of manufacturers now incorporate blaze orange into their hunting clothes, as well.

Boots seem to be the item given the least attention when it comes to noisemaking potential. Whatever kind of boots you wear—leather, rubber, fabric, you name it—it is difficult to

No matter what clothing you choose to hunt in, make sure it's comfortable and quiet in the field. (Rodney Schlecht)

keep them from sounding off against low-growing vegetation, unless you pull your pant legs down over the tops of them.

Another problem is the sound some boot soles make in "squeaky" snow. The popular, deeply-grooved and hard-rubbered soles seem to be the worst offenders. Flat soles, on the other hand, can be treacherously slippery. Lightly-patterned soles made of relatively soft rubber are best for both snow and dry-ground walking.

Where you walk, of course, has a great deal to do with how your feet are going to sound hitting the ground. For example, I was out recently looking for deer in weather I can't remember ever having at the end of October. The temperature was in the high sixties and there hadn't been rain in months, which made the forest noisy just to look at.

Nevertheless, I was able to move fairly quietly by following wood roads, fire trails, and well-used game trails. And I did see game, despite the comments of local hunters who thought it was crazy to be hunting on the move under such dry conditions.

SMELLS

When mule deer started getting into my garden several years ago, I spent $100 on materials and built an eight-foot-high fence. Some friends up the road had the same problem. But they spent only a few dollars to buy the cheapest, smelliest soap they could find. With a dozen bars of smelly soap hung around their garden, they've kept the muleys from their vegetables as effectively as I have with my tall, expensive fence.

Yes, I needlessly squander money at times, but more to the point: deer have discerning noses. They can detect and be repulsed, or frightened, not only by smelly soap, but by such items as aftershave lotion and scented antiperspirant. So, if you anoint yourself with pleasant-smelling products during or after a shower, it may be attractive to your sweetie, but it could raise hell with your hunting.

An unwashed body in dirty clothes may also do little to enhance your hunting. Any kind of smell, for that matter, that is not harmonious with a game animal's world will alert it to danger. So to start with you should make yourself and your hunting clothes as odorless as possible. Use unscented bath and clothes soap along with unscented antiperspirants. Dry your clothes in the open air if possible, and by all means, don't anoint yourself with anything.

According to some hunters, commercial hunting scents that imitate smells such as pine fragrance or scents that attract animals by imitating food smells such as apples are surefire game-getters. The same scents are pooh-poohed by other hunters. Objective opinion seems to indicate that these scents can be effective in some instances; at other times they are useless or even detrimental. Unfortunately, finding the situations and the conditions under which these scents will work still seems to be a hit-or-miss affair. Until the effects of these scents are more predictable, I opt for the no-smell approach.

While many clothing manufacturers now incorporate scent-blocking technology into everything from hunting shirts to boots, it is, of course, impossible to eradicate all smell from your body and clothes. So you'll still have to pay attention to the ways of the winds. Knowledge of the shifting nature of local winds will allow you to plan your general hunting movements ahead of time.

SILHOUETTE

Although the clothes you wear cannot hide your shadow or your silhouette, proper clothing can help you blend in with the surrounding countryside even in the full light of the midday sun. Camouflage clothing is certainly something you'd wear while bowhunting for mule deer and it can also be worn effectively and legally while rifle hunting. Although most states require rifle hunters to wear a specific amount of hunter orange above the waist (usually over 400 inches), regular camo clothing can be worn under an orange vest or you can even wear orange camo.

We tend to forget that deer see in shades of black and white. Since color is missing, it is the presence of contrast that becomes striking to their eyes, the same element that draws our attention to a particularly eye-catching black and white photograph. The effectiveness of blaze camo comes from the fact that the orange color lets other hunters see you, but the irregular blotches of black and gray overlying the orange break up your silhouette to the eyes of mule deer. So as silly as blaze orange camo may appear to other people, you can wear it while knowing that mule deer will have a hard time seeing you, even in bright sunlight.

Keep in mind that a camo or brown background doesn't mix well against the mono-color of a forest opening or against the unrelenting blue of an open sky. And not only must you pay attention to where you walk, but you should consider how you walk. Most big-game animals have eyes that are much more adept at identifying silhouettes that are on the move than those that are stationary. The faster and more erratic the movement, the more noticeable it becomes. So go slowly, and go with grace.

Remember, too, that bright sunlight can still bounce flashes of light off rings, watches, eyeglasses, or anything else you wear or carry that is shiny. One flash of light is enough to put deer on the run.

If Richard, Joe, and Charlie could sit down and tell their tales over a tall one on a Saturday evening, they'd probably become better hunters. For it's not just attention to your own smells, sounds, or silhouettes that matter—it's putting it all together that makes the difference.

SELECTING A RIFLE

Choosing a hunting rifle for mule deer can be as complicated as you want to make it. You can consult multitudes of experts, study reports, charts, and ballistics tables. You can read the stars and the cards and quiz friends, acquaintances, and complete strangers. You can agonize over half a dozen rifles, or even more. But selecting a rifle does not really have to be difficult.

I prefer to keep the whole process simple.

Start by considering the game you're after. A mule deer is bigger than a whitetail but not by much. Muleys run between 150 and 350 pounds. If you get into an exceptional buck, he may push 400 pounds—plenty hefty, but certainly not elephantine.

Also, consider the distances at which you're likely to be shooting. You may get shots at forest-dwelling mule deer that will be measured in dozens of yards. On the plains or in the desert, however, you might be shooting at deer that are hundreds of yards away. Still, the thrill of mule deer hunting, as I hope I've imparted in these pages, is in cultivating the ability and the know-how to get close to deer. With that in mind, any shot over 250 yards is a long shot—too long a shot in my book.

So what kind of rifle will you need to effectively down a 350-pound mule deer at 250 yards with one shot? I add the qualifier of a single shot because you'll want the deer on the ground after one shot. It may run fifty yards, even a hundred yards, on sheer adrenaline after it's shot, but it will most likely be running too fast to take pot shots at before it collapses. So think one shot, and when you do, you will also think about getting as close as you can to your game before you pull the trigger. That's a lot of what mule deer hunting should be about. So one shot is a good mindset with which to hunt.

A bolt-action rifle is perfect for that one shot. You aren't going to need the speed that other actions may offer for popping cartridges in and out. A bolt action is also more dependable and safer than other actions.

To further simplify your choice in a mule deer rifle, I'd select from one of these calibers: 7mm/08, .270, .280, or .30/06. And use a 140-grain cartridge with all of these except the .30/06, which should take a 150-grain cartridge. The .30/06 is more rifle than you'll need for mule deer in most situations, but I've used one for decades. There are, of course, many other rifles that will effectively take muleys, but we're keeping things simple.

A few more pointers: Stick with the standard 22-inch barrel on your deer rifle. And go for a synthetic stock over the more traditional wooden stock. Wood can twist, warp, swell, and shrink in weather that runs from dry to humid to soaking wet during the mule deer season. Those moisture changes can do disconcerting things to a rifle you thought was sighted-in perfectly.

Finally, a good deer rifle should have a good scope. Variable power scopes have become the standard these days. A modern 3X-9X scope will offer you a bright, full-field view of deer without a lot of head bobbing to find the exact position for clarity. You don't need any higher magnification than 9X (something like 2.5X-8X or 3X-10X is also fine), because as you go higher your in-focus range gets pushed out farther. For example, with an adjustable objective lens focused at 200 yards on a 14X scope, objects closer than 150 yards are going to be blurry.

Today, in the first years of the twenty-first century, a decent rifle/scope combination could end up costing $1,000 ($600–$700 for rifle, $300–$400 for scope). An indecent (i.e., real fancy) rifle/scope combo could run $3,000. But it's your money. You may already have a perfectly fine deer rifle, one you've used to hunt whitetail, for instance. So, you may not need to spend a dime.

When mule deer hunting, you can't go wrong with a synthetically stocked bolt-action .270, .280 or .30/06 with a variable scope.

There are, of course, alternatives to the modern deer rifle for hunting mule deer. If you are fanatical about deer hunting, and you are skilled with a bow, a modern rifle, and a muzzleloader, you can start hunting at the end of August in Colorado, for example, with a bow. Come October, you can switch to your rifle; in November take up your muzzleloader and in December go back to the bow. This may require that you move around the state or region a bit to follow the open seasons, but you could conceivably hunt for four months by taking advantage of the archery and blackpowder seasons, in addition to the regular rifle season.

As an archer, you'll have to bring into play your best skills and knowledge of muley habits and habitats to get close enough for an accurate shot—about thirty yards, let's say. A muzzleloader will give you a little more distance, 100 yards tops, but probably it's more realistic to think in terms of 50 to 75 yards.

Specialty magazines and books will help you go through the gyrations of selecting a suitable bow or blackpowder rifle. But remember, keep it simple. And whatever you use to go after mule deer, live by this motto: a clean kill with a single shot. You owe it to the deer you hunt.

ARE YOU READY FOR HUNTING SEASON?

It's time to ask yourself if you're ready to go hunting. Or to put it a bit more bluntly: Are you fat? Are you clumsy of foot? Has your eye dulled? Is your hand unsteady?

If you're honest, you've answered yes at least a couple of times, and you've said to yourself, I can use some help. So, here are some steps you can take to get in shape.

PHYSICAL SHAPE

I confess to having a passion for peanut butter and jelly on Saltine crackers. I get into them more often than I should. So I try to mitigate the size of the pot they put in my belly by walking at a brisk pace three miles a day. I'm about as manic over the walking as I am over the peanut butter and jelly crackers. Consequently, I've reached a kind of equilibrium with the two.

The point is that only you know how your body responds to your style of eating and exercise. So you'll have to be honest with yourself about how much tuning up you need. Generally, you should exercise in ways that put your body through movements that are similar to hunting conditions. Walking regularly uphill and down, two to three miles, three to four days a week, is a good place to start. If you have to walk in a gym, use a stair machine with a trainer's recommendations. You can also climb up and down stairs in your own home or apartment carrying weight that matches your hunting gear.

Don't neglect your upper body and your stomach. Pull-ups and push-ups will condition your arms for those off-hand shots you'll inevitably have to make. Sit-ups help tighten your stomach and, therefore, help relieve wear and tear on your lower back.

Be consistent about your exercises. Start doing them several months before hunting season if you don't simply work at keeping in shape all year.

SHOOTING SHAPE

First, sight-in your rifle to hit three inches high at 100 yards (see Chapter 30, Selecting a Rifle for more information on popular calibers for mule deer hunting), so you'll be right on target for an occasional long shot—250 to 300 yards. Then practice regularly with your rifle until you can consistently hit a 6-inch circle or square at 100 yards from the kneeling and standing positions.

Although it will help you to go to a regular target range and fire at stationary targets from various shooting positions, ideally you would practice on one of those walk-through ranges where targets appear out of the bushes, the kind recruits negotiate during their Army basic training. You can create your own simplified version by choosing a safe outdoor setting and placing three targets against an earth backdrop at different distances. Have a companion call out what target to shoot and from what shooting position. You may want to put a time limit on getting off a shot, ten seconds, say, or even five.

SKILLS IN SHAPE

The guy who spends all his time in a shop or office, only going into the field for a week or two each year, rarely slides right into skillful woodsmanship the minute he's on a hunt. He tends to walk too fast and with too much noise. He doesn't pay enough attention to signs of game, and he forgets how to see what's there to be seen. You may need some acclimation time in the woods remembering and practicing how to walk and observe. Perhaps you can get to your hunting destination a day or two early for this reason. Or maybe you can drive to the country — if you live in the city — and take some walks prior to a hunt.

TACTICS IN SHAPE

Hunting plans often go awry because the route you planned to hunt has become impassable with downfalls that you didn't know about. Or your neighbor and his buddies have swept through an area you wanted to hunt just before you got there.

Getting your hunting tactics in shape means planning and scouting. You need to check to see that hunting routes are passable and that the area is currently being used by game. You need to check with other hunters who you know will be using the same area in order to coordinate your tactics.

GEAR IN SHAPE

To assure myself that my equipment is ready for the hunting season, I perform what I call the "dry run." Two weeks before the season opens, I deck myself out in exactly what I plan to carry and wear while I'm hunting. I mean I start from my birthday suit and work out—socks, underwear, all the way to fanny pack, granola bars, and rifle.

To help in this process, I have a list tacked on the wall in the back room. I won't amuse you with what I feel compelled to wear or carry. Besides, you can make up your own personal list of can't-do-withouts, including things that I might be happy to leave at home.

Anyway, after I'm fully laden with all the things on my list, I parade around in them for ten or fifteen minutes. I walk up and down the stairs or out in the yard to get a feel for things and to listen for any unwanted squeaks or taps or clinks. The squeaky heel of a boot gets a day with the cobbler. The socks that seem too bulky are replaced with thinner ones. The pack whose straps have miraculously shrunk over the summer get adjusted to fit around the extra pork chops.

Once everything feels and sounds right, I take it all off, one item at a time, checking each item carefully as it is shed. Does the knife need sharpening or the sheath need repair? Are the binoculars clean of dog slobber and do they adjust properly? Does the zipper work on the pack? Are there any holes in my pockets? Do my boots need waterproofing? Is my dragline too frayed for another season?

I take this routine quite seriously. And only when I've taken off and examined the last sock and I'm standing bare-bunned (to my wife's laughter) do I know I'm ready to hunt.